The Language of Science Education

The Language of Science Education

*An Expanded Glossary of Key Terms and
Concepts in Science Teaching and Learning*

Edited by

William F. McComas
*Parks Family Professor of Science Education,
University of Arkansas, Fayetteville, AR, USA*

SENSE PUBLISHERS
ROTTERDAM / BOSTON / TAIPEI

A C.I.P. record for this book is available from the Library of Congress.

ISBN 978-94-6209-495-6 (paperback)
ISBN 978-94-6209-496-3 (hardback)
ISBN 978-94-6209-497-0 (e-book)

Published by: Sense Publishers,
P.O. Box 21858, 3001 AW Rotterdam, The Netherlands
https://www.sensepublishers.com/

Cover photo:
The cover photo was taken by W.F. McComas at Marsh's Library in Dublin, Ireland. This amazing library houses more than 25,000 rare and important books including many related to the history of science. It was founded in 1701 and has remained essentially unchanged for three centuries. Permission to use this image as the cover for *The Language of Science Education* has been granted by Dr. Jason McElligott, Keeper of Marsh's Library.

Printed on acid-free paper

PREFACE AND INTRODUCTION

As science education has matured as a discipline, it has developed experts in the field, specialized journals, professional meetings, advanced degree programs along with a unique language and the desire on the part of scholars and practitioners from across the globe to participate in work designed to enhance science teaching and learning. Recently, these last two elements came together when I was approached by colleagues from the *Excellence Research Center of Science and Mathematics Education* (ECSME) of the King Saud University in Riyadh, Saudi Arabia. Their request was to write a glossary defining a number of key terms within science education so that they could more fully understand the literature and make contributions to it. This immediately seemed to be a worthy and interesting project with potentially far reaching implications to promote shared understanding.

The original list of more than seventy terms featured an important cross section of many aspects of science education, all of which were worthy of formal definition. The list revealed that science education has truly developed its own language with unique entries and general education terms contextualized with respect to science teaching and learning. It was immediately clear that knowledge of this core set of terms would be fundamental to having shared and productive conversations within the discipline. As we completed our task for ECSME, they graciously encouraged us to expand the work and produce a product directed at a wider audience.

With this opportunity before us, we next called upon members of the science education community to review the list of terms already defined and suggest those we may have missed. In just a few days, more than forty individuals offered approximately sixty additional terms for consideration. The task of determining which ones should be included was made relatively easy by noting that many additional words were suggested by multiple individuals. Therefore, this edition of *The Language of Science Education* contains one hundred unique terms related to practice and research within the discipline of science education.

Readers will note that each term is accompanied by two definitions. First, a quick and easily accessible one appears at the top of each page followed by a more extensive narrative with examples and further commentary. The definition of most terms has been restricted to a single page so this did not become an encyclopedia, but a few words such as such as laboratory, constructivism and inquiry ultimately required additional space. In some cases, minor terms related to the main one are included there so that readers could easily see relationships without having to flip back and forth throug the book. Also, links are provided to refer readers to related terms using the note "see also" wherever applicable

Although one hundred unique terms are defined, the many synonyms and links included expand the list considerably. For those looking for a specific definition, simply begin by consulting the table of contents. However, readers may find it interesting to peruse the definitions as they appear in alphabetical order; you may be surprised, as we were, by the precision, complexity and variety of the vocabulary used in the study of science teaching and learning. We anticipate that readers will encounter some unfamiliar terms and form some new understandings just by reading the book as if it were a collection of short (very short) stories, and we encourage doing so.

The definitions provided are those that would be embraced by the majority of those in science education without introducing new and unfamiliar terms. However, in several cases, it was not possible to follow this rule. For instance, the term "science education" has historically been defined so vaguely that it often appears as a synonym for "science teacher" and this simply is not reasonable given the differences in the work of those who identify themselves as science educators. "Interdisciplinary instruction" is problematic. If we consider the term discipline as a "way of knowing," it is reasonable to offer a new term, "blended science instruction" as a more accurate substitute. Finally, there is the challenge of "problem based" vs. "project based" instruction. The new scholarship regarding "project based" does offer a nice distinction between the two modes of learning but few seem to attend to this distinction. We hope that readers will consider issues such as these with an open mind knowing that we welcome any feedback.

It will be clear that the vocabulary of science education and key documents from the United States are somewhat over-represented in this set of one hundred key terms related to science teaching and learning, but we look forward to addressing this situation in future editions of the book. We sincerely welcome suggestions for enhancement and expansion (and correction) that may come from those who review this first edition of *The Language of Science Education*.

I would like to thank friends and colleagues at the *Excellence Research Center of Science and Mathematics Education* who inspired this project, most particularly Dr. Hiya Al-mazroa who first contacted me with this intriguing opportunity. I would also like to thank all of those associated with the *Program to Advance Science Education* at the University of Arkansas who assisted with the writing and editorial tasks, specifically doctoral student Ms. Charlie Belin who used her superb organizational skills to keep the project on track. She also contributed her artistic talents to produce the diagrams and illustrations included to support several of the definitions. Finally, I acknowledge a debt of gratitude to Dr. Michael Clough of Iowa State University and Dr. Allison A. Meyer of Illinois State University who read each line and made countless suggestions resulting in a final product far better than would have been possible without their extraordinary assistance.

Fayetteville, Arkansas
September 2013

ACKNOWLEDGEMENT

The editor acknowledges and appreciates the support of colleagues from the Excellent Research Center of Science and Mathematics Education in the production of this book.

The Excellence Research Center of Science and Mathematics Education

CONTRIBUTING AUTHORS

The development of this book has been a productive partnership between graduate students, faculty members and others who contributed the definitions found here. Although each term has been closely edited, each of the primary authors can be identified by the inclusion of their initials at the conclusion of each entry.

Readers and authors should recognize that the editor occasionally engaged in significant rewriting for clarity, space considerations and readability and therefore takes full responsibility for the content, accuracy and format of the final definitions presented here.

AB	Amy Baeder	KM	Kim Murie
AR	Adnan Al-Rubaye	LA	Leonard Annetta
CB	Charlie Belin	LW	Lisa Wood
CW	Cathy Wissehr	PW	Peggy Ward
JH	Jacob Hayward	SI	Silvia Imanda
JK	John Kester	WM	William McComas

SUGGESTED REFERENCE FORMAT

Readers may be interested in referring to the author initials found at the end of each definition to credit the appropriate author. Here is an example of how the definition for advance organizer might be cited.

Ward, P. (2014). Advance organizers. In W. F. McComas (Ed.), *The language of science education* (p. 4). Boston: Sense Publishers.

TABLE OF CONTENTS

5E Inquiry Model (See Learning Cycle) 59
21st Century Skills 1
Academic Language in Science 2
Academic Standards (see Standards) 101
Action Research 3
Advance Organizer 4
Alphabet Soup Science Curriculum Projects 5
Analogies in Science Teaching 6
Argumentation in Science Teaching 7
Atlas of Science Literacy 9
Authentic Inquiry (see Inquiry Instruction) 52
Authentic Science Learning Contexts 10
Backing (see Argumentation) 7
Benchmarks in Science Teaching (General Definition) 11
Benchmarks for Science Literacy (U.S. Document) 12
"Big Ideas" in Science (see Crosscutting Concepts) 28
Blended Science Instruction 13
Classroom Discourse 15
Claims (see Argumentation) 7
Cognitive Dissonance (Disequilibrium) 16
Collaborative Inquiry Learning (see Inquiry Instruction) 52
Coordinated Science Instruction (see Blended Science Instruction)... 13
Common Core Standards (U.S. Document) 17
Computer Simulations 18
Concept Map 19
Conceptual Change Teaching (see Constructivism) 21
Conceptual Profile 20
Conceptual Understanding.. 105
    (see Teaching for Conceptual Understanding)
Coordinated Science (see Blended Science Instruction) 13
Constructivism as Learning Theory 21
Constructivist Teaching Practices 23
Construction of Scientific Knowledge 24
Context-based Science Education 25
Controversial Scientific Issues in Science Teaching 26
Cookbook Laboratory (see Laboratory and Science Teaching)......... 55
Core (see Disciplinary Core Ideas) 37
Critical Thinking 27
Crosscutting Concepts 28
Culturally Relevant Pedagogy (CRP) 29

Curriculum 30
Deductive Thinking (See also Induction) 31
Diagnostic Assessments 32
Didactic Instruction 33
Differentiation (Differentiated Instruction) 34
Discovery Learning (Teaching) 35
Disequilibrium (see Cognitive Dissonance) 16
Discrepant Event 36
Disciplinary Core Ideas 37
Dry Lab (see Laboratory) 55
Epistemology and Epistemological Beliefs (see Nature of Science)... 67
Environmental Education 38
Ethics in Science 39
Experiential Learning 40
Experiments (see Laboratory and Science Teaching) 55
Evidence (see Argumentation) 7
Framework for K-12 Science Education (U.S. Document) 41
Frameworks (General Definition)... 42
Foundation for Unified Science Education (FUSE) 13
    (see Blended Science Instruction)
Formative Assessment (see also Summative) 43
Globalization of Science Education 44
Grounds (see Argumentation) 7
Guided Inquiry (see Inquiry Instruction)................................... 52
Hands-on Science 45
Hypothesis (Scientific Hypothesis) 46
Hypothetico-deduction... 47
Inclusive Science Instruction 48
Induction (Inductive Thinking) (see also Deduction) 49
Inferences (Inferring in Science) 50
Informal (Free Choice) Science Learning 51
Inquiry Continuum (see Inquiry Instruction) 52
Inquiry Instruction 52
Integrated Science (see Blended Science Instruction) 13
Intradisciplinary Science Instruction... 13
    (see Blended Science Instruction)
Interdisciplinary Science Instruction... 13
    (see Blended Science Instruction)
Laboratory and Science Teaching 55
Laboratory Experiments (see Laboratory and Science Teaching)...... 55
Laboratory Levels of Inquiry 55
    (see Laboratory and Science Teaching)
Law (Scientific Law or Principle) 58
Learning Cycle 59
Learning Progression 61

Meaning Making and Science Learning 62
Metacognition 63
Micro-computer Based Laboratory (MBL) 64
Misconceptions (Alternative Conceptions) 65
National Science Education Standards (U.S. Document) 66
Nature of Science 67
Next Generation Science Standards (U.S. Document) 69
Open Inquiry (See Inquiry Instruction) 52
Outdoor Science Education 70
Pedagogical Content Knowledge (PCK) 71
Pedagogical Practices in Science Teaching 72
Place-based Learning 73
Prerequisite Knowledge and Skills (see Prior Knowledge) 74
Prior Knowledge in Teaching and Learning 74
Probes and Probeware 75
Problem Based Learning (PBL) 76
Problem Solving 77
Process Skills (see Science Process Skills) 89
Process Oriented Guided Instruction (POGIL) 78
Programme for International Student Assessment (PISA) 79
Project 2061 (U.S. Science Education Program) 80
Project-based Instruction (PBI) 81
Puzzling Phenomenon (See Discrepant Event) 36
Questioning Strategies 82
Radical Constructivism (see Constructivism) 21
Rebuttal (see Argumentation) 7
Reasoning (see also Argumentation) 83
Rhetoric of Science (see Scientific Discourse)........................... 91
Scaffolding 84
Science and Engineering Practices 85
Science Education 86
Science Fairs, Exhibitions, and Research Competitions 87
Science Notebooks (Notebooking) 88
Science Process Skills 89
Science, Technology and Society (S/T/S) 90
Scientific Discourse (Rhetoric of Science)............................... 91
Scientific Hypothesis (see Hypothesis) 46
Scientific Literacy 92
Scientific Method (Scientific Methodology)............................. 93
Scientific Model (Modeling)... 94
Scientific Openness 95
Scientific Principle (see Law/Principle) 58
Scientific Theory (see Theory) 107
Scientific Thinking Skills 96
Scientific Writing Heuristic (SWH) 97

Situated Learning 98
Social Constructivism 99
Socio-scientific Issue-based Instruction 100
Standards (Academic Standards) in Science Teaching................. 101
Structured Inquiry (See Inquiry Instruction) 52
STEM: Science, Technology, Engineering, and Mathematics 102
Summative Assessment (see also Formative Assessment) 104
Teaching for Conceptual Understanding 105
Technological Pedagogical Content Knowledge (TPACK) 106
Theory in Science (Scientific Theory) 107
Trends in International Mathematics and Science Study (TIMMS)... 108
Unified Science Instruction (see Blended Science Instruction) 13
Urban Science Education 109
Virtual Learning Environments 110
Virtual Laboratory (see Laboratory and Science Teaching) 55
Warrant (see Argumentation) 7
Wet Lab (see Laboratory and Science Teaching)........................ 55

"21st-Century Skills" is a term frequently used to define what students should know and be able to do to enter the workforce and make decisions in the modern world. Supporters of this idea suggest that schools should be more concerned with what students can do with knowledge rather than the amount of knowledge itself.

There is no single set of "21st-Century Skills" and hundreds have been suggested. Many lists include life skills (agility, flexibility, and adaptability), workforce skills (collaboration, leadership initiative, and responsibility), applied skills (accessing and analyzing information, effective communication, and determining alternative solutions to problems), personal skills (curiosity, imagination, critical thinking, and problem solving), interpersonal skills (cooperation and teamwork), and non-cognitive skills (managing feelings) (adapted from Saavedra & Opfer, 2012).

The National Science Teachers Association's (2011) "21st-Century Skillset" includes "core subject knowledge; learning and innovation skills; information, media, and technology skills; life and career skills; adaptability; complex communication and social skills; non-routine problem solving; self-management/self-development; and systems thinking" (p. 1).

While many of the "21st-Century Skills" have been around for years, there is now a push to teach them at every educational stage because success in the modern world depends on having these skills (Silva, 2009; Bybee & Fuchs, 2006; Rotherham & Willingham, 2009; Stuart & Dahm, 1999). Opponents claim the term is meaningless and a distraction from teaching more traditional content knowledge. Silva (2009) offers a compromise and suggests that "students cannot develop and use these skills without a core body of knowledge" (p. 632).

The success of the "21st-Century Skills" movement depends on preparing teachers to effectively deliver both skills and content. To encourage acquisition of 21st-century skills, time to practice them and appropriate curriculum experiences must be provided. In addition, classroom tests and state assessments should be aligned with the content goals and delivered using coherent curricula (Silva, 2009; Rotherham & Willingham, 2009). (CB)

Bybee, R. W., & Fuchs, B. (2006). Preparing the 21st century workforce: A new reform in science and technology education. *Journal of Research in Science Teaching, 43*(4), 349-352.

National Science Teachers Association. (2011). Quality science education and 21st century skills. Arlington, VA: Author. Retrieved from
http://www.nsta.org/about/positions/21stcentury.aspx

Rotherham, A. J., & Willingham, D. (2009) 21st century skills: The challenges ahead. *Educational Leadership, 67*(1), 16-21.

Saavedra, A. R., & Opfer, V. D. (2012). Learning 21st century skills requires 21st century teaching. *Phi Delta Kappan, 94*(2), 8-13.

Silva, E. (2009). Measuring skills for 21st century learning. *Phi Delta Kappan, 90*(9), 630-634.

Stuart, L.m & Dahm, E. (1999). *21st century skills for 21st century jobs.* Washington, DC: United States Department of Commerce.

Academic Language in Science is the formal, precise terminology used in discipline-or domain-specific ways by those fluent or literate in that discipline. In addition to subject-specific academic language, there is also general academic language that cuts across disciplines that students use to engage in reading, writing, speaking, and listening tasks.

The use of academic language in science is addressed in the *Common Core State Standards* (see also) for English Language Arts. For example, Standard 4 of Science and Technical Subjects for grades 11-12 states that students should be able to "Determine the meaning of symbols, key terms, and other domain-specific words and phrases as they are used in a specific scientific or technical context relevant to grades 11–12 texts and topics" (Council of Chief State Officers, 2010). Science teachers, therefore, must become supporters of academic language learning as students navigate these new terms, phrases, symbols, and patterns of discourse while working to gain proficiency in the content area. This will require science teachers to examine the curriculum and resources for the academic language that is present, incorporate literacy strategies into lessons, and provide opportunities for students to exercise their academic language fluency through listening, reading, writing, and speaking. These literacy strategies will benefit all students but will be critical for students learning academic language in addition to conversational English.

Additionally, in order to assist students in meeting the *Next Generation Science Standards* (Achieve, 2013) (see also), teachers are encouraged to emphasize the use of academic language in classroom discourse and learning. Lee et al. (2013) suggest that teachers promote academic language acquisition through "supporting students' ability to do things with language, engaging them in purposeful activities, and providing them with opportunities for language use" using "task based instruction" (p. 6). They also suggest that because engagement with the NGSS's science and engineering practices requires the intensive use of academic language, science teachers must "encourage and support language use and development in the service of making sense of science" (p. 231). In conclusion, as students use science-specific academic language in both productive and receptive ways, their fluency will increase as they move toward being scientifically literate. (AB)

Achieve, Inc. (2013). *The Next Generation Science Standards.* Retrieved from http://www.nextgenscience.org/next-generation-science-standards.
Lee, O., Quinn, H., & Valdes, G. (2013). Science and language for English language learners in relation to *Next Generation Science Standards* and with implications for common core state standards for English language arts and mathematics. *Educational Researcher, 42*(4), 223-233.
Council of Chief State School Officers. (2010). *Common core state standards: English language arts standards initiative.* Washington, DC: Author. Retrieved from http://www.corestandards.org/

Action Research is a kind of limited research study (also called *practitioner research, practitioner led research,* and *practitioner-based research*) (McNiff et al., 2003) conducted by teachers, counselors, principals, and others in a teaching/learning environment for the purpose of gathering information about how to improve instructional practices and student learning outcomes and to affect positive changes in that specific educational environment (Mills, 2003).

Whereas much traditional educational research is conducted by researchers who are not embedded in the environment in which the research is taking place, action research (AR) is conducted by practitioners with the primary intention of improving their classroom practices. Therefore, AR has both a personal and a social purpose. The personal purpose is to improve the skills of the practitioner, and the social aim is to improve some situation. The limited and focused nature of the study means that the results may not be applicable to environments beyond the one where the data were collected. When compared with traditional research, AR is designed to impact practice immediately and its purpose is local rather than to learn things that have more generalized application. Action researchers choose their own focus, determine their research methods and data collection techniques, analyze and interpret their data, and develop action plans based on their findings (Mills, 2003; McNiff et al., 2003).

Myka and Raubenheimer (2005) investigated the impact of increasing the level of intellectual challenges by redesigning four laboratory activities in a section of a university laboratory class. The original activities included observations of slides and preserved specimens as well as group dissections, while the redesigned activities were altered so that students in those classes would engage in observations of animals, develop a dichotomous key, and do some exercises in classification and model building. The participating students completed both the traditional laboratory activities as well as the four redesigned activities during the two semesters of the course. To assess the effectiveness of the redesigned laboratory, the researchers conducted a survey to analyze student perceptions, to understand their learning and enjoyment for all the laboratory exercises, and to determine if students' impressions of learning were associated with their performance (Myka & Raubenheimer, 2005). In keeping with the purpose of AR, the instructor planned future activities based on the findings of this research.

The best teachers will always question how they are doing in the classroom and conducting "action research" investigations will help them judge their effectiveness and answer other questions of interest within the classroom context. (PW)

Mills, G. E. (2003). *Action research: A guide for the teacher researcher* (2nd ed.). Upper Saddle, NJ: Pearson.

Myka, J. L., & Raubenheimer, C. D. (2005). Action research implemented to improve zoology laboratory activities in a freshman biology majors course. *Electronic Journal of Science Education, 9*(4), 1-27.

McNiff, J., Lomax, P., & Whitehead, J. (2003). *You and your action research project* (2nd ed.). New York, NY: Routledge Falmer.

Advance Organizers are instructional activities or strategies that are used before teaching to help students think about and organize the information they are about to learn and help them to connect prior knowledge to the new information they are about to encounter (Woolfolk, 2011).

Advance organizers may be presented in written forms such as handouts, charts and diagrams, concept maps, or they may begin instruction in the form of specific pre-discussions, stories, films, visuals, and computer software presentations. An advance organizer could be an opportunity for students to explore the environment or the equipment that will be studied formally. Likewise, metaphors, similes and models might also be used as advance organizers (see analogy). Advance organizers are typically teacher constructed due to the nature of their use. Organizers generally serve three purposes: they focus students' attentions to what is coming; they highlight relationships among ideas that will be presented, and they help students make connections between what they already know and the new information to be learned (Woolfolk, 2011). Consider this example of an advance organizer for student preparing to learn about the periodic table in chemistry class. Students might be given a copy of the periodic table and asked to think about what they already know about it, explore it, make some predictions about how it might be organized, ask questions about why the elements appear in rows and columns, and to write down any thoughts they have or questions they would like to ask.

Also, advance organizers can help students retain unfamiliar but meaningful verbal information by relating the new material to existing cognitive structures (Woolfolk, 2011). Studies also show that using advance organizers may enhance learners' motivation to learn (Shihusa & Keraro, 2009). Effective instructors must take time to ensure that students understand the organizer such as having students paraphrase it, and the organizer must make connections to the basic concepts that will be learned and the terms that will be used (Woolfolk, 2011).

The use of advance organizers as tools of effective learning and retention has been widely debated (Chen, 2007). Although the research shows that advance organizers are not equally effective for all learners in all situations, Ausbel (1978) suggests that the effectiveness of advance organizers depends upon the age of the learner, the nature of the subject, and the degree of prior familiarity with the material to be learned. (PW)

Ausbel, D. P. (1978). In defense of advance organizers: A reply to the critics. *Review of Educational Research, 48*(2), 251-257.

Chen, B. (2007). Effects of advance organizers on learning and retention from a fully web-based class. (Doctoral dissertation). Retrieved from:
http://etd.fcla.edu/CF/CFE0001556/ Chen_Baiyun_200705_PhD.pdf

Shihusa, H., & Keraro, F. N. (2009). Using advance organizers to enhance students' motivation in learning biology. *Eurasia Journal of Mathematics, Science & Technology Education, 5*(4), 413-420.

Woolfolk, A. (2011). *Educational psychology* (11th ed.). Boston, MA: Allyn & Bacon.

Alphabet Soup Science Curriculum Projects is the informal name for the vast number of science teaching projects sponsored by the U.S. government in the 1960s, such as those in physics (PSSC), chemistry (CHEM study), biology (BSCS) and elementary education; ESS, S-APA and others. These acronym-rich names gave rise to the label "alphabet soup" projects and curricula.

In the midst of the Cold War, the U.S. federal government expressed concern about the apparent Soviet superiority in science and technology following the successful satellite launch of *Sputnik* in October 1957. A year later the National Defense Education Act (NDEA) was signed along with an increase in funding from the National Science Foundation to enhance educational innovations in schools and universities at a variety of levels and institutions.

Experts from groups such as the Division of Physical Science of the National Academy of Science, the Association of Physics Teachers and the National Science Teachers Association (DeBoer, 1991) were already meeting to address concerns about science instruction. These groups established committees to study education in each of the major science disciplines including the Physical Science Study Committee (PSSC), Biological Science Curriculum Study (BSCS), Chemical Education Material Study (CHEM), and Earth Science Curriculum Project (ESCP). These curriculum study groups and others proposed a staggering number of formal curriculum projects generally focused on how to communicate to student both the products and processes of science. These curricula generally integrated laboratory activities into instruction, minimized the cookbook (see also) nature of science labs, emphasized higher cognitive skills and focused on student understanding of the nature of science (Kyle et al., 1983). There is no single list of such projects but included major curricula like S-APA (Science – A Process Approach), ESS (Elementary Science Study), CBA (Chemical Bond Approach), SCIS (Science Curriculum Improvement Study) and many others with similar "alphabet" names, including some developed later.

Studies (Kyle et al., 1983; Bredderman, 1983) showed positive impacts when some of these "alphabet soup" projects were compared with traditional instruction particularly where intensive professional development was provided but none of these projects now exist in their original forms. Critics complained that some of the projects were too focused on content while others failed to provide enough, they demanded too much of schools and teachers in terms of training and materials, and/or required external funding that did not remain available. In spite of their demise, these projects impacted teaching significantly by introducing inquiry at all instructional levels and demonstrating the efficacy of kit-based programs. (WM)

Bredderman, T. (1983, Winter). Effects of activity-based elementary science on student outcomes: A synthesis. *Review of Educational Research, 53*(4), 499-518.

DeBoer, G. E. (1991). *A history of ideas in science education: Implications for practice.* New York: Teachers College Press.

Kyle, W., Shymansky, J., & Alport, J. (1983). The effects of new science curricula on student performance. *Journal of Research in Science Teaching, 20*(5), 387-404.

Analogies in Science Teaching are those examples teachers use to make difficult concepts more understandable by using something familiar to teach something that is unfamiliar. A common science teaching analogy is to compare electricity in a circuit to water flowing in the pipes in a house.

Analogies may be in the form of metaphors, similes, examples, and visual representations used during instruction to compare what the student already knows with new information the student will learn (Venville & Treagust, 1997). For example, biology teachers often suggest that the cell is a factory and the organelles are the components of the factory (i.e. the mitochondrion as the "powerhouse" of the cell and ribosomes as protein factories). Other examples include the structure of DNA as a twisted ladder, and Darwin's branching tree to represent evolution
   A typical analogy has two parts, the source (familiar to students) and the target (less familiar). For instance, teachers may refer to the heart as a pump and the flow of electricity as similar to water in a pipe. In these two cases, the "sources" in the analogies are the pump and flowing water because these are more familiar concepts. The "targets" are heart function and the movement of electrons as the less familiar concepts that we want students to understand.
   Analogies are also used to motivate students by provoking their interests and to help students restructure their knowledge frameworks by making the unknown more understandable. Before using an analogy in the classroom, the strength and usefulness must be considered and must be based on how accurately it relates one concept to another and the prior knowledge and experiences of the students for whom it is intended (Dagher, 2004). In some cases, students can grasp a particular concept without the use of analogies. In other situations, some students will benefit from one particular analogy while other students need different ones. The use of analogies should be constantly assessed and based upon students' background knowledge, their experiences, and their needs. Good analogies must be personally and culturally relevant to students. For instance, if a science teacher uses an analogy about a sport such as cricket that is not known to her students, the analogy might be ineffective or even cause confusion.
   There is some conflicting research regarding the use of analogies in the classroom (Venville & Treagust, 1997). Analogies used carelessly may cause confusion and even promote student misconceptions (Dikmenli, 2010). Therefore, caution should be exercised to ensure students learn about and remember the concept and not just the analogy. Teachers must be skilled at recognizing the strengths and weaknesses of analogies used during instruction. (PW)

Dagher, Z. R. (2004). The case for analogies in teaching science for understanding. In J. J. Mintzes, J. H. Wandersee, & J. D. Novak (Eds.), *Teaching science for understanding: A human constructivist view* (pp. 1965-211). San Diego, CA: Academic Press.
Dikmeli, M. (2010). An analysis of analogies used in secondary school biology textbooks: Case of Turkey. *Eurasian Journal of Educational Research, 10*(4), 73-90.
Venville, G. J., & Treagust, D. F. (1997). Analogies in biology education: A contentious issue. *The American Biology Teacher, 59*(5), 282-287.

Argumentation in Science Teaching is a way in which individuals and scientists engage in a discussion to examine ideas and evidence and offer a logical debate (argument) regarding whether, for a given circumstance, ... a proposed explanation is consistent or not with some observation" (Duschl et al., 2007. p. 33). Argumentation is increasingly recommended for inclusion in science instruction.

Argumentation, including scientific argumentation, is a process of discussion and debate designed to uncover "as much information and understanding from the situation under discussion as possible." With the added notion that "alternative points of view are valued as long as they contribute to this process within the accepted norms of science and logic, but not when they offer alternatives ... outside those norms" (p. 33). A growing number of documents (American Association for the Advancement of Science, 1993; National Research Council [NRC], 1996, 2007) recommend including argumentation as part of science instruction so that students can learn how to engage effectively in the skills of argumentation.

The NRC's (2011) *Framework for K-12 Science Education* identifies the ability to engage in argument as one of eight central scientific practices. One cannot do science unless one is familiar with the process of arguments, because "... science is replete with arguments that take place both informally ... and formally ... Regardless of the context, both scientists and engineers use reasoning and argumentation to make their case" (pp. 3-17). The new U.S. *Common Core State Standards* asks students to "delineate and evaluate the argument and specific claims in a text, including the validity of the reasoning as well as the relevance and sufficiency of the evidence" (Council of Chief State Officers, 2010).

The basic elements of formal argumentation (claim, warrant and backing) were defined by Stephen Toulmin (1958/2003) in *The Uses of Argument*. However, a number of synonyms have been proposed making the language of argumentation surprisingly complex.

The argument itself is the relationship between the information put forward to support a *claim* and the *claim itself.*

Claim (assertion or proposition) offered by the individual making the argument; the notion at the center of the debate.
Warrant, is the inferential leap connecting the claim with the backing. Warrants are typically based on authority, logic such as induction or deduction, emotional appeals and shared values.
Backing or Evidence (grounds, support) are the facts put forward to convince others engaged in the argument itself.
Rebuttals are the counter-points offered by others designed to refute the evidence and defeat a particular argument.

In Toulmin's framework it is difficult to capture the different levels and layers of student reasoning, to identify what is evidence, data, and backing, and to determine "the extent to which reasoning is-or should be-content independent or content embedded" (Brown et al., 2010, p. 132). In response Brown et al. developed the Evidence-Based Reasoning Framework (EBR) (see also reasoning) as "... a description of using theoretical statements, backed by scientific evidence, to evaluate the quality of a claim." It is not a model of "how scientific knowledge is or should be generated by students or scientists" (p. 132). (JH/CB/WM)

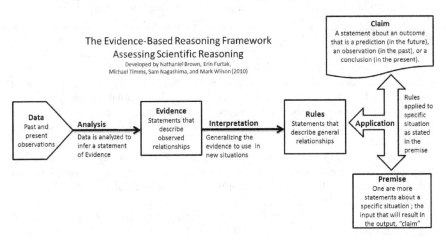

American Association for the Advancement of Science. (1993). *Benchmarks for science literacy.* New York: Oxford University Press.

Brown, N. J. S., Furtak, E. M., Timms, M., Nagashima, S. O., & Wilson, M. (2010). The evidence-based reasoning framework: Assessing scientific reasoning. *Educational Assessment, 15*(3/4), 123-141.

Council of Chief State School Officers. (2010) *Common core state standards initiative.* Washington, DC: Author. Retrieved from http://www.corestandards.org/

Duschl, R. A., Schweingruber, H. A., & Shouse, A. E. (Eds.). (2007). *Taking science to school: Learning and teaching science in grades K-8.* Washington, DC: National Academic Press.

National Research Council. (1996). *National science education standards.* Washington, DC: National Academy Press.

National Research Council. (2011). A *framework for K-12 science education: Practices, crosscutting concepts, and core ideas.* Washington, DC: National Academies Press.

Toulmin S. E. (2003/1958). *The uses of argument, updated edition.* Cambridge, UK: Cambridge University Press.

The *Atlas of Science Literacy* is a collection of over 100 "maps" based on Project 2061's *Benchmarks for Science Literacy* (see also) that depict how students' literacy in science, mathematics, and technology likely develops as students mature throughout their years in school. Such "maps" are also called learning progressions.

The *Atlas of Science Literacy* is published by the American Association for the Advancement of Science (AAAS) and is separated into two volumes. The first volume, published in 2001, primarily focuses on how students across grades K-12 can increase their scientific literacy knowledge base. The second volume, published in 2007, expanded on the first volume but was primarily focused with helping all Americans "form a coherent understanding of the world and how it works." For example, it includes a map regarding learning concepts linked to weather and climate, a human development map, and an evolution explanation map. Both volumes include maps that are accompanied by commentary on the facing page, that provides an overview of the main topic, the content of the map and the major corresponding strands with chapters in *Benchmarks*, the learning focus at each of four grade ranges, and notes that might be of interest to the readers (AAAS, 2007; National Science Teachers Association, 2013).

According to AAAS, each *Atlas* can be used by educators to better understand benchmarks and standards, design curriculum, plan instruction, develop and evaluate curriculum materials, construct and analyze assessment, prepare teachers, and organize resources. The maps are not intended to advocate a particular instructional strategy but to pose a framework that will inspire creativity in the design and organizing of curriculum as best suited for any individual student, classroom, school, district, or state (AAAS, 2013).

Researchers and curriculum designers may also use the Atlas's to determine learning goals, pinpoint student misconceptions, and to create additional conceptual maps. Krajcik et al. (2007) used the *Atlas* to provide create the pedagogical perspectives necessary to inform curriculum units. Their maps focused on "project-based pedagogy, such as the need to connect to students own experiences and contextualize the units in real problems" (p. 6). (CB)

American Association for the Advancement of Science. (2007). *Atlas of science literacy completes mapping of science-learning pathways.* Washington, DC: Author. Retrieved from http://www.aaas.org/news/releases/2007/0329science_atlas.shtml
American Association for the Advancement of Science. (2013). *Atlas of science*, Volumes 1 and 2. Mapping K-12 science learning. Washington, DC: Author. Retrieved from www.project2061.org/publications/atlas/default.htm
Krajcik, J., McNeill, K. L., & Reiser, B. J. (2007). Learning-goals-driven design model: Developing curriculum materials that align with national standards and incorporate project-based pedagogy. *Science Education, 92*(1), 1-32.
National Science Teachers Association. (2013). *Atlas of science literacy*, volume 1. Arlington, VA: Author. Retrieved from
    http://www.nsta.org/store/product_detail.aspx?id=10.2505/9780871686688

Authentic Science Learning Contexts are learning experiences closest to being the most authentic (realistic) that thus provide students an opportunity to engage in the real-work of scientists in real-world or highly realistic situations (Braund & Reiss, 2006).

Traditional science teaching usually gives students a false view of how science functions in the real world. If students had an opportunity to see scientists at work they would understand that scientific processes (see scientific process skills) are more complex and more interesting than what is typically shown in school. Although it may be possible for teachers to produce authentic learning experiences in the classroom, many such experiences will occur outside the school. For instance, students working in a laboratory at a local university or industry or serving as an intern on a research project with zoologists or veterinarians at the zoo would have the opportunity to experience science in the most authentic context.

Authentic science learning implies that students are exposed to a more accurate picture of how science is done by experiencing science as scientists do (see discovery learning) rather than what they would see from traditional classroom instruction. Authentic science learning means that students engage in self-directed tasks, open-ended inquiries, and learn the role of debate and argumentation (see also) in places outside of the classroom (Braund & Reiss, 2006) while practicing it in the classroom.

An authentic approach shifts the focus from traditional content taught in regular classrooms to places or situations that relate to the science content being presented. In all cases authentic science practice allows students to experience the tools and techniques, social interactions, and attitudes of science (Edelson, 1997). In authentic approaches students learn there are specific tools and techniques used by scientists. Students will also learn that although scientists share certain standards of scientific inquiry there is no prescribed set of steps by which all scientists conduct investigations (see scientific method).

Students also need to know the importance of communication and social interactions as it pertains to authentic science. Scientists rarely work in isolation and often confer with others or build from the ideas of others. Finally, it is important for students to understand that there is uncertainty in science; it is characterized by the pursuit of the unknown. Allowing students to explore science in the real-world (the most authentic of situations) or by engaging in real inquiry in a classroom setting can help students see science in the most real or authentic way possible. In doing this students will become more keen observers of the natural world, begin to ask personally relevant questions, and understand the true nature of science. (KM)

Braund, M., & Reiss, M. (2006). Towards a more authentic science curriculum: the contribution of out-of-school learning. *International Journal of Science Education, 28*(12), 1373-1388.

Edelson, D. (1997). Realising authentic science learning through the adaptation of scientific practice. In K. Tobin & B. Fraser (Eds.), *International Handbook of science education.* Dordrecht, The Netherlands: Kluwer.

Benchmarks in Science Teaching are specific content standards of what students should know, understand, and be able to do at specific grade levels (Parkay et al., 2010). Benchmarks can be used to develop performance standards (see also), assessment tools, textbooks and instructional plans. Some consider "benchmarks" and "standards" to be the same, but benchmarks are more general goal statements while standards are more specific.

A well-known example of a document containing benchmarks is *Benchmarks for Science Literacy* (see also) (American Association for the Advancement of Science, 1993). This U.S. document was designed to provide statements about what all students should know and be able to do in science, mathematics, and technology by the end of grades 2, 5, 8, and 12. The recommendations at each grade level suggest reasonable progress toward delineated goals of science literacy as defined in *Science for all Americans* (Rutherford & Ahlgren, 1990).

Benchmarks are like standards in that they specify what students should know and be able to do; however, unlike standards, benchmarks also indicate when (what grade level) and what performance levels students should be able to understand and/or perform the standard. In some settings, student performance levels, or benchmarks, are defined in terms of "advanced," "proficient," "basic," and "below basic." Those who develop the measures of assessment determine the levels of performance students must achieve to reach one of these levels.

Benchmark exams may be administered during the school year and are used to determine if schools are doing well or if they are falling short of the desired outcomes as established in the benchmark documents. For example, in the U.S., schools are deemed to be in distress (low-performing) because too many students are scoring below the expected level, they may receive funds and other assistance to help them create and implement improvement plans. If these schools continue to demonstrate inadequacy, they could be sanctioned or even taken over administratively. Additionally, media scrutiny may provide motivation for school districts to make the necessary improvements in order to meet the minimum requirements. (PW)

American Association for the Advancement of Science. (1993). *Benchmarks for science literacy.* New York, NY: Oxford University Press.
Parkay, F., Anctil, E. J., & Hass, G. (2010). *Curriculum leadership: Readings for developing quality educational programs* (9th ed.). Boston, MA: Allyn & Bacon.
Rutherford, F. J., & Ahlgren, A. (1990). *Science for all Americans.* New York, NY: Oxford University Press.

Benchmarks for Science Literacy is a document developed by the American Association for the Advancement of Science containing a recommended set of science learning goals or benchmarks (see also) specifying what students should know and be able to do in science, mathematics, and technology by the end of Grades 2, 5, 8, and 12 (American Association for the Advancement of Science [AAAS], 1993).

Benchmarks emerged after a three year research study sponsored by the AAAS called Project 2061. This name is inspired by Halley's Comet which was last seen in 1985 when work began on the project. It relates to the scientific and technological changes children entering school in 1985 might expect to see before the comet returns in 2061.

Benchmarks is a companion publication to *Science for all Americans* (Rutherford & Ahlgren, 1991), which specifies what students should be able to know and do in science, math, and technology by the time they graduate from high school. *Benchmarks* build on what is contained in *Science for all Americans* and provides helpful checkpoints along the way to estimate student progress to achieving scientific literacy goals (AAAS, 1995).

Benchmarks does not provide a curriculum but is a set of targets that curriculum designers, textbook authors and teachers would use to meet the goals for science literacy as recommended in *Project 2061* (AAAS, 1995). *Benchmarks* emphasizes levels of understanding and abilities that all students are expected to reach as they progress toward becoming scientifically literate. *Benchmarks* does not advocate any particular teaching methods but the U.S. National Science Education standards (see also) strongly recommend inquiry as a teaching method.

Two examples of the Nature of Science *Benchmarks* are listed below:

- By the end of the 8th grade, students should know that "when similar investigations give different results, the scientific challenge is to judge whether the differences are trivial or significant, and it often takes further studies to decide ..." (AAAS, 1993, p. 7).
- By the end of the 12th grade, students should know that "... when applications of research could pose risks to society, most scientists believe that a decision to participate or not is a matter of personal ethics rather than professional ethics" (AAAS, 1993, p. 19). (PW)

American Association for the Advancement of Science. (1993). *Benchmarks for science literacy.* New York, NY: Oxford University Press.

American Association for the Advancement of Science. (1995). *Project 2061: Science literacy for a changing future, a decade of reform.* Washington, DC: Author.

Rutherford, F. J., & Ahlgren, A. (1991). *Science for all Americans.* New York, NY: Oxford University Press

Blended Science Instruction is an umbrella term proposed by McComas and Wang (1998) as a way to label and then clarify integrated, interdisciplinary and unified science instructional approaches. Blended science is any instructional plans that features content from a combination of sciences (biology and chemistry, for instance) or science and non-science disciplines (biology and the humanities, for instance) together. This new term is recommended because of the lack of precision inherent in existing labels provided below.

Any definition of instructional proposals that reach beyond a single domain such as biology must begin with a discussion of the concept of the discipline. Disciplines are unique "ways of knowing" with their own "rules" and traditions. Phenix (1964) recognized a range of such "ways of knowing" with labels such as empirics (science), symbolics (mathematics), aesthetics (arts), ethics, synnoetics (literature) and synoptics (history).

Intradisciplinarity, strictly speaking is the mingling of content from within a single "way of knowing" such as represented by the empirical pursuit known as science. Therefore, a course that blends content from physics and chemistry would best be characterized as an intradisciplinary science course. Advocates for intradisciplary science instruction remind us that modern science is increasingly interdisciplinary and collaborative with problems solved by those from across the individual disciplines. Traditional disciplines have been integrated into new specialty areas such as biogeochemistry, genetic engineering, nanoscience, systems biology, and biotechnology all which require foundations in more than one science discipline. So, an integrated approach to teaching science provides students with a more accurate view of nature itself and a more accurate picture of how science functions in the modern world.

Integrated Science is closely related to the intradisciplinary approach. Richmond (1974) and *The United Nations Educational, Scientific, and Cultural Organization* define integrated science as "those approaches in which concepts and principles of science are presented so as to express the fundamental unity of scientific thought and to avoid premature or undue stress on the distinctions between the various scientific fields" (p. 46). Some forms of integrated science instruction do involve areas outside of the sciences resulting in a potentially confusing definition for the term.

Unified Science, though similar to integrated science, does not typically include links to disciplines outside of science. Victor Showalter and his colleagues were among the first advocates for this type of science teaching and developed a large number of instructional units through FUSE, the *Foundation for Unified Science Education*. Typically, these units centered on a theme, like water pollution, and involved all of the sciences in an exploration of that theme. The unified science units included characteristics of science that could be found in all of the individual

13

science subjects every student should learn as well as common facts and concepts (Showalter, 1973).

Coordinated Science is a formal instructional approach to support intradisciplinary science teaching. It was developed by the *National Science Teachers Association* to "cut through the layer cake" of the typical secondary school approach to science in which students take a discrete science class each year (Aldridge, 1992; Aldridge et al., 1997). Coordinated science differed from both integrated and unified approaches because it specified the way in which instruction should be organized to enhance blending. Topics of instruction in each science discipline would be taught in a spiral approach with each topic revisited yearly at higher levels of thinking (McComas & Wang, 1998).

Interdisciplinary Science, when the term is used in the most precise fashion with reference to Phenix (1964), represents science teaching that strategically links "science as a way of knowing," to some other way of knowing such as may be found in mathematics, the arts or humanities. In other words, instruction that connects science and at least one non-science disciplines (McComas, 2009). Scientists and philosopher C.P. Snow (1959) in his landmark book, *The Two Cultures*, provides the most succinct rationale for interdisciplinary instruction. In this book he described what he saw as a gulf separating those engaged in science and those with a worldview grounded in some other "way of knowing." Snow believed that bridging this gap would provide more opportunities for shared understanding and more ways to solve the problems of the modern world. (WM)

Aldridge, B. G. (1992). *Scope, sequence, and coordination of secondary school science, Volume I: The content core: A guide for curriculum designers.* Washington, DC: National Science Teachers Association Press.

Aldridge, B. G., Lawrenz, F., & Huffman, D. (1997). Scope, sequence, and coordination: Tracking the success of an innovative reform project. *The Science Teacher, 64*(1), 21-25.

McComas, W. F. (2009). Thinking, teaching, and learning science outside the boxes. *The Science Teacher, 76*(2), 24-28.

McComas, W. F., & Wang, H. A. (1998). Blended science: The rewards and challenges of integrating the science disciplines for instruction. *School Science and Mathematics, 98*(6), 340-348.

Phenix, P. H. (1964). *Realms of meaning: A philosophy of the curriculum for general education.* Venture, CA: Irving S. Sato Printing Company.

Richmond, P. E. (Ed.). (1974). *New Trends in integrated science teaching: Education of Teachers. Volume III.* Paris, France: United Nations Educational, Scientific, and Cultural Organization.

Snow, C. P. (1959). *The two cultures.* London: Cambridge University Press.

Classroom Discourse refers to the conversation that occurs between teachers and students in the classroom including both verbal and nonverbal exchanges (Cazden & Beck, 1998).

Learning generally involves speech. Teachers communicate with students verbally and students demonstrate what they have learned using spoken language. Typically, teachers talk more than two-thirds of the time, with the remainder of time being spent on individual students answering questions posed by the teacher (Nuthall, 1997). Those who have studied classroom discourse have noticed that boys talk more than girls, and that students sitting front and center generally contribute most frequently. Findings such as these can help inform teachers about the role and nature of classroom discourse and may be used to improve practice.

Researchers have identified three main patterns of classroom discourse. The first is *student silence* because the teacher talks the majority of the time and only occasionally asks questions. The second pattern of classroom discourse is *controlled*; teachers ask questions, but they are usually predetermined and have one correct answer. The final pattern is *active*; this is where a teacher acts as the facilitator with the main interaction occurring between the students (Alpert, 1987).

In all classrooms language is important as a way of allowing students to explore their ideas and formulate their thinking. In a science classroom, this language is even more important since science is about discovery. Teachers must be aware of the classroom discourse taking place and try to shift the momentum so that students are the ones primarily engaged in the talking as opposed to the teacher.

This may be accomplished through improved questioning strategies (that require more than a yes or no answer, for example) used by teachers and employing wait time (pausing after asking a higher order question). However, even these strategies may be insufficient in immediately enhancing classroom discourse. When students are asked to respond in front of their peers, this may be intimidating. It is important to create a supportive classroom climate, maintain good non-verbal behaviors (like smiling, eye contact and raising eyebrows to show interest) and accepting responses from students rather than quickly evaluating them as valid or not. (Clough et al., 2009). (KM)

Alpert, B. R. (1987). Active, silent and controlled discussions: Explaining variations in classroom conversation. *Teaching and Teacher Education, 3*(1), 29-40.

Cazden, C. B., & Beck, S. W. (2003). Classroom discourse. In A. C. Graesser, M. A. Gernsbacher, & S. R. Goldman (Eds.), *Handbook of discourse processes*. Mahwah, NJ: Lawrence Earlbaum Associates.

Clough, M. P., Berg, C. A., & Olson, J. K. (2009). Promoting effective science teacher education and science teaching: A framework for teacher decision-making. *International Journal of Science and Mathematics Education, 7*(4), 821-847.

Graesser, A. C., Gernsbacher, M. A., & Goldman, S. R. (Eds.). (2003). *Handbook of discourse processes* (pp. 165-197). Mahwah, NJ: Lawrence Erlbaum Associates.

Nuthall, G. A. (1997). Understanding student thinking and learning in the classroom. In B. J. Biddle, T. L. Good, & I. F. Goodson (Eds.), *International handbook of teachers and teaching*, Vol. II (pp. 681-768). Dordrecht, The Netherlands: Kluwer Academic Publishers.

Cognitive Dissonance, or *disequilibrium*, is the discomforting mental state that students enter when their predictions and explanations conflict with what they have just seen, heard or experienced (Piaget, 1978). Learners make sense of the world by applying what they already know, believe, or remember (sometimes called their conceptual framework) and when this framework is at odds with reality, dissonance can result.

If there is a discrepancy between the student's existing schema or framework and the learning experience, several things may occur. Students may 1) not recognize the discrepancy, 2) simply ignore it, 3) explain it away, 4) hold two conflicting ideas or 5) may call into question their current ideas. All of these states have important implications for teaching and learning. Cognitive dissonance prompts students to take one of three actions: changing their existing beliefs or ideas, adding new ideas to bridge the two conflicting beliefs, or reducing the importance of one of the dissonant elements.

Since learners naturally want to experience cognitive equilibrium, when teachers employ lessons that introduce cognitive dissonance, students' motivation to learn may be increased. We want students to feel dissonance or disequilibrium when the new facts fail to fit students' current understands. As a result of this dissonance, students will likely exhibit information-seeking behavior (Festinger, 1957), which can be harnessed by classroom teachers.

The optimal state is for students' faulty conceptions to be challenged so that the most scientifically valid idea replaces those that are less valid. Unfortunately, students may hold two conflicting beliefs or ideas about how the world works, one for school and one for personal use. In such cases, noting the students' correct response on an assessment provide no assurance of what students really think.

Science teachers should work to promote and resolve dissonance with their students. If cognitive dissonance is introduced repeatedly and students are not successful at attaining equilibrium due to poorly implemented sense-making activities or a lack of well-scaffolded lessons (see also), students can lose motivation. Students need help accessing and interpreting new information so they can make connections between their new ideas and their overall schemata.

Science teachers can prompt cognitive dissonance or disequilibrium by a demonstration, a laboratory or other hands-on activity, a video, or the introduction of a discrepant or puzzling event (see also). When students realize that their existing views are inadequate to explain their experience, they begin to look for other explanations. Students create "mini-theories" as they learn more, and they test those mini-theories against the original experience to see if there is a fit resulting in more equilibrium or less dissonance (Appleton, 1993). (AB/WM)

Appleton, K. (1993), Using theory to guide practice: Teaching science from a constructivist perspective. *School Science and Mathematics, 93*(5), 269-274.
Festinger, L. (1957). *A theory of cognitive dissonance.* Stanford, CA: Stanford U. Press.
Piaget, J. (1978). *The development of thought: Equilibration of cognitive structures.* Oxford: Blackwell.

The *Common Core Standards* is a set of learning goals sponsored by the United States' National Governors Association (NGA) and the Council of Chief State School Officers (CCSSO) prescribing what students in grades K-12 are expected to learn in mathematics and English Language Arts literacy. The science curriculum is impacted because *Common Core* recommends related literacy goals.

In 2009, the NGA hired the company *Student Achievement* to develop curriculum standards that are "robust and relevant to the real world, reflecting the knowledge and skills that our young people need for success in college and careers" (CCSSO, 2010, p. 1). These standards were designed to prepare students to compete successfully in the global market. During 2012-13, 45 of 50 states had implemented the recommendations of the *Common Core* (CCSSO, 2010).

Although *Common Core* primarily provides standards for the teaching of mathematics and English Language Arts, they also support science instruction and other subjects by defining content literacy. These literacy standards will not replace content standards but supplements them by addressing particular challenges in reading, writing, speaking, listening, and language in the major academic fields.

The ELA-Literacy strands for science are divided into three different grade ranges: 6-8, 9-10, and 11-12. Each grade range has 10 science standards organized by four different categories: Key Ideas and Details, Craft and Structure, Integration of Knowledge and Ideas, and Range of Reading and Level of Text complexity. Some examples of standards from the 9-10 grade range include:

- KEY IDEAS and DETAILS: Cite specific textual evidence to support analysis of science and technical texts, attending to the precise details of explanations or descriptions (CCSS.ELA-Literacy.RST.9-10.1)
- CRAFT and STRUCTURE: Analyze the structure of the relationships among concepts in a text, including relationships among key terms (e.g., *force, friction, reaction force, energy*) (CCSS.ELA-Literacy.RST.9-10.5)
- INTEGRATION of KNOWLEDGE and IDEAS: Compare and contrast findings presented in a text to those from other sources (including their own experiments), noting when the findings support or contradict previous explanations or accounts (CCSS. ELA-Literacy.RST.9-10.9) (CCSSO, 2010). (CB)

Council of Chief State School Officers (CCSSO). (2010). Common core state standards initiative. Washington, DC: Author. Retrieved from http://www.corestandards.org/

Computer Simulations in science education refer to the use of a computer or other digital device to recreate the steps and/or results of an actual scientific investigation or to demonstrate or model aspects of some natural phenomenon.

Simulations may be used by the teacher for illustration purposes or may be used by students to conduct a laboratory activity on the computer. Such laboratory simulations are typically used where the actual supplies may be expensive or unavailable, where the procedure is dangerous, or where it makes instructional sense to run the procedure or analysis many times and doing so in a classroom setting would be impractical and time consuming. Of course, simulations using computers are also very useful in science fields such as biology, physics, astrophysics, social science, and engineering. For instance, climate scientists use powerful computers to produce models of the atmosphere and make predictions about future climate patterns. Such predictions would not be possible without the use of computers because of the vast number of variables involved. Students can also explore science in similar ways using classroom versions of simulations designed for scientific investigation.

In science and science teaching, simulations are useful only if they accurately show the phenomenon in question and/or produce the same results that would otherwise be obtained by doing an actual investigation. Therefore, creating accurate computer simulations requires much prior information and the results of real-world investigations and observations (Hunter & Naylor, 1970).

Geban and colleagues (1992) conducted a study on high school students to check the effect of using computer simulation on students' interest toward chemistry instruction, chemistry achievement results, and students' knowledge of the scientific process. The researchers found that using a computer simulation approach positively impacted students' achievement in the chemistry class when compared to the didactic instruction (see also) lacking such simulations. Also, using computer simulation improved students' attitude toward studying biochemistry. Gokhale (1996) found that incorporating computer simulation into lecture-based labs improves students' performance and can motivate students' self-discovery abilities which improve students' overall understanding of the class material and their final results. (AR)

Geban, O., Askar, P., & Ozkan, I. (1992). Effects of computer simulations and problems solving approaches on high school students. *Journal of Educational Research, 86*(1), 5-10.
Gokhale, A. A. (1996). Effectiveness of computer simulation for enhancing higher order thinking. *Journal of Industrial Teacher Education, 33*(4), 36-46.
Hunter, J. S., & Naylor, T. H. (1970). Experimental designs for computer simulation experiments. *Management Science, 16*(7), 422-434.

Concept Map is a pictorial representation of the links and the relationship between ideas held by learners regarding particular scientific ideas or phenomenon. These representations may be drawn by students themselves or by teachers while interviewing students (Halford, 1993). Such pictures are useful to learners in expressing what they already know and to teachers in assessment and in developing instruction that builds on knowledge of students' preexisting ideas.

The ability to organize thoughts and illustrate them is a valuable cognitive skill for all learners. Developing this capacity is vital to the students' potential to gain from classroom instruction. For the sciences in particular, a broad range of concepts exist that encompasses a complex web of interrelationships students must comprehend to fully understand the content. Students use concepts to guide the thinking process. When concept mapping, a concept is listed in either a box or a circle. Then each concept is connected to another by a line or arrow. This displays a relationship between concepts and represents a progression in the thought process.

As an example, consider the following concept map developed by young students who were asked to think about what the sun provides to the Earth:

In this very basic concept map, the sun is the main focus with two major effects. The arrows point to light and heat equally showing that the student believes that the sun emits these two types of energy. A concept map can include text written by the student to

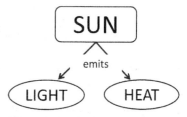

accompany the arrows and explain the nature of the relationship (Sun *emits* heat). These are known as linking phrases that further develop the visualization of the concept map (Novak & Cañas, 2006).

This simple concept map portrays the foundational understanding that is now illustrated in a clear and concise format both for teachers and students. Of course, many concepts maps are far more complex and have many boxes (concepts) and relationships (linking lines).

Potential applications for concept mapping are endless, but it is best utilized as a complementary strategy for science instruction (Kinchin & Hay, 2000). The broad applicability and visual characteristics make the concept map a vital tool Students who use concept maps for studying have been shown to improve their study skills and in learning science lessons (Kinchin & Hay, 2000). (JK)

Halford, G. S. (1993). *Children's understanding: The development of mental models.* Hillsdale, NJ: Lawrence Erlbaum.

Kinchin, I. M., & Hay, D. B. (2000). How a qualitative approach to concept map analysis can be used to aid learning by illustrating patterns of conceptual development. *Educational Research, 42*(1), 43-57.

Novak, J. D., & Cañas, A. J. (2006). *The theory underlying concept maps and how to use them.* Pensacola, FL: Florida Institute for Human and Machine Cognition.

Conceptual Profile is the idea "that people can exhibit different ways of seeing and representing the world, which are used in different contexts" (Mortimer, Scott, El-Hani, 2012, p. 234). Conceptual profiles are useful tools in a science classroom setting when considering students' different ways of thinking, analyzing classroom conversation, and in linking thought processes and talking. Mortimer (1995) developed the idea of "conceptual profile" as an extension of Bachelard's (1940/1968) epistemological profile.

Conceptual profile theory is based on knowing something of the learners' "concept." The concept is the mental model that exists in the mind of an individual. Concepts occur in the mind of the individual through a dynamic process called conceptualization or conceptual thinking (Mortimer et al., 2012). Schutz (1967) and Tulviste (1991) argued that individuals have different ways of experiencing, seeing, and conceptualizing the world, part of the premise behind conceptual profile theory.

So, such concepts belong solely to each individual learner and are relatively stable mental units. "Conceptual profiles are built for a given concept and are constituted by several zones, each representing a particular mode of thinking about that concept, related to a particular way of speaking. As would be expected, each individual has his or her own individual conceptual profile" (Mortimer et al., 2012).

For example, in everyday life when dealing with behavior and properties of solid substances, a "continuous view" of matter is sufficient. However, an individual could draw on a different perspective such as the "quantum view" of matter, the theory that matter displays both particle-like and wavelike properties; or the "atomistic view," the theory that matter is composed of discrete unites called atoms. Both the "quantum view" and the "atomistic view" are quite different from the "continuous view," the theory that everything was composed of long uninterrupted, continuous blobs of matter that can be divided over and over again without limit. However, if these three different perspectives are combined, it could reveal one's conceptual profile of a *solid*. The learner can refer to and use any one of these views under different circumstances or contexts (Mortimer, 1995). (CB)

Bachelard, G. (1968/1940). *The philosophy of no.* (G.C. Waterston, Trans.) New York, NY: Orion Press.

Mortimer, E. F. (1995). Conceptual change or conceptual profile change? *Science and Education, 4*(3), 265-287.

Mortimer, E. F., Scott, P., & El-Hani, C. N. (2012). The heterogeneity of discourse in science classrooms: The conceptual profile approach. In B. J. Fraiser, K. G. Tobin, & C. J. McRobbie (Eds.), *Second international handbook of science education* (pp. 231-246). Dordrecht/New York: Springer.

Schutz, A. (1967). *Der sinnhafte Aufbau de sozialen Welt* (The phenomenology of the social world). New York, NY: Northwestern University Press.

Tulviste, P. (1991). *The cultural-historical development of verbal thinking.* New York: Nova Science.

Constructivism refers to a number of related ideas in learning theory that share the notion that individuals must develop (or construct) understanding based on their prior experiences and personal interaction with objects and ideas and with other individuals. Constructivism has a number of distinct meanings so care must be taken when using this term (Woolfolk, 2011; Matthews, 1998).

Constructivism as Learning Theory emphasizes the active role of the learners during the processes of constructing their own understanding (Woolfolk, 2011) based on experiences and reflections of those experiences. Constructivism implies personal knowledge construction as opposed to simple knowledge transmission (Applefield et al., 2001).

To understand the idea of constructivism and the power of pre-existing knowledge, consider trying to convince a child who believes the Earth is flat (this is called a misconception or alternative conception) that it is actually round. The child immediately visualizes a flat but round pancake-shaped Earth. When told the Earth is spherical, the child may visualize a sphere with their flat pancake shaped Earth on top of it and with people standing on top of that. In order to help the child to overcome these misconceptions and begin to develop an accurate sense of a spherical Earth, the child's misconceptions must first be recognized (both by the teacher and the child) and then addressed appropriately (Bransford et al., 2000).

Although there is no single constructivist theory of learning, most constructivists agree on two core ideas: that learners are active in constructing their own knowledge and that social interactions are an important part in the construction of knowledge (Woolfolk, 2011). In a classroom guided by constructivist learning theory, students are responsible for tackling problems and making sense of experiences, they share ideas with their peers and teacher, and the teacher performs a vital role in the learning process by interacting with students in scaffolding their thinking and providing information when needed. Teachers also must be aware of students' prior knowledge and use this information in designing lessons and asking questions of students (Gordon, 2009).

While most science educators find some value in the use of constructivism in the classroom, Matthews (1998) rejects pedagogy based on constructivist learning theory. He asks, "Why must learners construct for themselves the ideas of potential energy, mutation, linear velocity ... Why not explain these ideas in such a way that students understand them?" (p.9). However, because learners will use their prior understanding to make sense of teachers' explanation, teachers must acknowledge that it is the learners who must make meaning for themselves.

Conceptual Change Teaching is instruction based on the idea that students' pre-existing knowledge can either support or interfere with future understanding. There is no single model called "conceptual change teaching" but several of the learning cycle models (see also) are based on constructivist principles since they give students (and teachers) an opportunity to think about what students already know (Tabachnick & Zeichner, 1999).

The idea behind conceptual change teaching is the basic recognition on the part of the teacher that students' prior ideas play a role in future understanding. If the prior concepts held by students are not accurate they are called misconceptions or alternative conceptions (see also). Such misconceptions therefore must be used in the classroom and changed through instruction. Therefore, the name "conceptual change" relates to the expectation that students already have concepts (perhaps inaccurate) that must be changed or replaced by ideas that are more scientifically appropriate (Duit & Tregust, 2003). Teaching for conceptual understanding (see also) is related to conceptual change teaching since the goal of school science instruction is that students will fully understand the concept or idea not just know it at a shallow level.

Even though this book focused on the vocabulary of education, there is a form of philosophical constructivism that often enters the conversation and, therefore, demands a place here.

Radical Constructivism is an extreme form of constructivism suggesting that there is no reality or truth in the world. Therefore, "truth" is deemed as that which an individual perceives and believes (Woolfolk, 2011). Such a view implies an "anything goes" form of instruction (Gordon, 2009) and that students should have opportunities to direct their own learning, follow their own interests, ask the questions they want answers to, and pursue their own meanings. Few educators would agree with the use of radical constructivism as a rationale for teaching and learning; learners could argue that whatever they learn is exactly what they wanted and needed to learn and hence they should not be guided by standards designed by nor should they be evaluated by assessments prepared by others. (PW/WM)

Applefield, J. M., Huber, M., & Moallem, M. (2001). Constructivism in theory and practice: Toward a better understanding. *The High School Journal, 84(*2), 35-53.
Bransford, J. D., Brown, A. L., & Cocking, R. R. (Eds.). (2000). *How people learn: Brain, mind, experience, and school.* Washington, DC: National Academy Press.
Duit, R., & Treagust, D. F. (2003). Conceptual change: A powerful framework for improving science teaching and learning. *International journal of science education, 25*(6), 671-688.
Gordon, M. (2009). Toward a pragmatic discourse of constructivism: Reflections on lessons from practice. *Educational Studies, 45*(1), 39-58.
Matthews, M. (Ed.). (1998). *Constructivism in science education: A philosophical approach.* Dordrecht, The Netherlands: Kluwer Academic.
Tabachnick, B. R., & Zeichner, K. M. (1999). Idea and action: Action research and the development of conceptual change teaching of science. *Science education, 83*(3), 309-322.
Woolfolk, A. (2011). *Educational psychology* (11th ed.). Boston, MA: Pearson.

Constructivist Teaching Practices are those pedagogical tools and decisions based on an application of constructivism (see also) as a learning theory (sometimes call Constructivist Learning Theory or CLT). The basic notion is that learners must be active participants in the development and construction of their own knowledge and must make their own meaning of information and experiences in order to gain personal understanding. There is no single set of constructivist teaching practices.

Constructivism implies teaching techniques based on the notion that students' prior knowledge profoundly impacts their understanding of subject matter, that students learn best when they apply knowledge in authentic contexts, engage in dialogue with their peers and others, and should strive for understanding of core ideas as opposed to memorizing and repeating a list of facts (Windschitl, 1999).

There are many models of teaching based on CLT and all agree that students' thinking and their efforts to understand must be at the center of effective instruction. Applefield et al. (2001) name four central components of teaching and learning based on constructivist learning theory:

1. Students construct their own knowledge and must be given opportunities to do so, not just to listen to their teachers;
2. New learning is dependent upon the students' prior knowledge, so teachers must know what students already have in mind and design lessons appropriately;
3. Knowledge is socially constructed so students should be given opportunities to work with others to discuss what they know and what they are thinking; and
4. Teachers must provide authentic learning tasks in order for learning to be meaningful. In other words, students must find the learning tasks personally relevant and linked to topics and processes in the real world

Teachers who use constructivist practices promote learning experiences that require students to be active participants in the learning process. Windschitl (1999) asserts "such experiences include problem-based learning, inquiry activities, dialogues with peers and teachers that encourage making sense of the subject matter, exposure to multiple sources of information, and opportunities for students to demonstrate their understanding in diverse ways" (p.752). In order to address the many different ways students may choose to explore within the discipline, constructivist teachers must have an intellectual grasp of the subject matter as well as a flexible understanding with a repertoire of multiple representations to help students understand the nature of the content (Windschitl, 1999). (PW)

Applefield, J. M., Huber, M., & Moallem, M. (2001). Constructivism in theory and practice: Toward a better understanding. *The High School Journal, 84*(2), 35-53.
Windschitl, M. (1999). The challenges of sustaining a constructivist classroom culture. *Phi Delta Kappan, 80*(10), 751-757.

Construction of Scientific Knowledge refers to learners' meaning-making based on personal experiences and reflections on those experiences as well as social interactions (see Constructivism, Social Constructivism and Conceptual Change Teaching for additional related information).

The idea that individuals develop or construct understanding is based on a constructivist theory of learning. In constructivism knowledge is not transmitted directly from one knower to another intact, but is interpreted by the learner so that knowledge becomes personal understanding (Driver et al., 1994). A wide range of research traditions supports the notion that learners make meaning with respect to scientific knowledge.

Personal construction of meanings and the informal ideas that individuals develop about natural phenomena result from personal interactions with events in daily life (Carmichael et al., 1990). Therefore, robust learning is enhanced in the classroom through well-designed practical activities that challenge prior conceptions and require students to rearrange their personal ideas based on these new experiences. Activities that are inquiry-based, problem-based, project-based, and/or place-based are common strategies for promoting the extensive mention engagement requirement for scientifically valid meaning making.

A second tradition suggests that scientific knowledge is constructed by learners when they are introduced to the language and processes of science (Lemke, 1990). The personal construction of knowledge relies heavily on the physical experiences and their role in learning science whereas a social constructivist perspective suggests that learning involves being introduced to a symbolic world. In this way knowledge and understanding are constructed when individuals engage socially in talk and activity about shared problems and tasks (Driver et al., 1994).

Construction of scientific knowledge by students is based on two main ideas which have their roots in constructivist learning theory. First, the learners are active in constructing their own knowledge. They do this through personal experiences and their interactions with objects and ideas. Second, social interactions are an important part of the construction of knowledge (Woolfolk, 2011). Classrooms designed to facilitate the construction of scientific knowledge are places where "individuals are actively engaged with others in attempting to understand and interpret phenomena for themselves, and where social interaction in groups is seen to provide the stimulus of differing perspectives on which individuals can reflect" (Driver et al., 1994, p. 7). It seems clear that the teacher's role with respect to students' knowledge construction is to promote thought and reflection as student transform information into personal knowledge. (PW)

Carmichael, P., Driver, R., Holding, B., Phillips, I., Twigger, D., & Watts, M. (1990). *Research on students' conceptions in science: A bibliography*. Leeds, UK: Centre for Studies in Science and Mathematics Education, University of Leeds.

Driver, R., Asoko, H., Leach, J., Mortimer, E., & Scott, P. (1994). Constructing scientific knowledge in the classroom. *Educational Researcher, 23*(7), 5-12.

Lemke, J. (1990). *Talking science*. Norwood, NJ: Ablex.

Woolfolk, A. (2011). *Educational psychology* (11th ed.). Boston, MA: Pearson.

Context-based Science Education (CBSE) and context-based learning (CBL) are new names for what has long been known as "problem-based learning" and now seem to be used interchangeably. In these approaches students study scientific concepts within the frame of reference (context) in which the scientific principles function. The name change was made to avoid the negative implication of the word "problem" which really just means "issue" in this case.

In problem-based learning (see also), a central feature of instruction is to give students a "problem" or issue within some real-world context or situation. An example of such a problem might be for students to explore what sort of effects different kinds of detergents have on the environment. As students explore this issue, they will learn many science principles such as the water cycle, eutrophication, algae growth, pollution, etc.

In a context-based classroom, the applications of science are presented first and then the scientific concepts to support those applications are examined. The idea is for the scientific ideas to be developed from the applications rather than to be defined only by the concepts (Bennett et al., 2007).

A number of science related curricula have been developed using a problem-based or context-based focus. Examples of this approach include *Biology: A Community Context (BioCom)* and *Chemistry in the Community* (*CHEMCom*) in the USA, *Salters Chemistry* in the UK and *Chemie im Kontext* in Germany (DeJong, 2008). Context-based science education has considerable overlap with many forms of the Science Technology and Society (S/T/S) teaching approach (see also) (Yager, 1996).

Supporters of this approach find that students' attitudes toward science are improved, there is a strong foundation provided for further scientific study, and students become more engaged in learning (Fensham, 2009). While on the other hand, there may be concern that not all relevant or important scientific concepts will be taught if an appropriate context cannot be found or constructed and the role such approaches play in creating literate citizens. (KM)

Bennett, J., Lubben, F., & Hogarth, S. (2007). Bringing science to life: A synthesis of the research evidence on the effects of context-based and STS approaches to science teaching. *Science Education, 91*(3), 347-370.

DeJong, O. (2008). Context-based chemical education: How to improve it? *Chemical Education International, 8*(1), 1-7.

Fensham, P. J. (2009). Real world contexts in PISA science: Implications for context-based science education. *Journal of Research in Science Teaching, 46*(8), 884-896.

Yager, R. E. (1996). *Science/technology/society as reform in science education.* Albany, NY: State University of New York Press.

Controversial Science Issues are scientific topics that, by their very nature, create discussions, debates, and questions because students are intrigued by these issues, question them or even have significant doubts about them. Such issues are useful in science teaching because students have opinions and are passionate about these topics.

Concepts, such as evolution, stem cell research, clone research, climate change, and the existence of great lengths of geologic time may conflict with students' personal, religious, or political views and ideologies causing discomfort, uncertainty, denial, or changing in one's thinking based on the data or facts presented. Incorporating controversial topics into science courses can create concern for teachers in how to present these topics.

Several resources have been produced, with the support of the U.S. National Science Teachers Association (NSTA) to provide educators with historical background knowledge, content knowledge, and instructional strategies and questions for use in class. Slesnick (2004) has created a resource called *Clones, Cats, and Chemicals: Thinking Scientifically about Controversial Issues* describing real-world events and experiences that incorporates different controversial issues. In one lesson example, Slesnick defines the topic of cloning, explains how it occurs naturally in a botanical context, when a leaf may break off and grow into an identical plant. There are examples to be found in the animal kingdom as well.

The use of controversial issues may present interesting and profitable instructional opportunities as in science, technology and society (S/T/S) (see also), and socio-scientific instruction. These issues can be used to increase student comprehension of science concepts, along with developing abilities to debate orally such topics. Cannard (2005) discusses the positive impact on student understanding of and learning about science concepts by investigating controversial science topics. Cannard suggests that students engaged in the study of controversial subjects need to develop an understanding of multiple viewpoints, be able to argue the various positions, and have "civic decision making" (p. 15) capabilities.

The National Science Teachers Association has produced a series of position statements available at http://www.nsta.org/about/positions.aspx#list to provide some additional background of various controversial issues which may be found at the NSTA website. (JH)

Cannard, K. (2005). Embracing controversy in the classroom. *Science Scope, 28*(9), 14-17.
Slesnick, I. (2004). *Clones, cats, and chemicals: Thinking scientifically about controversial issues*. Alexandria VA: National Science Teachers Association Press.

Critical Thinking refers to the ways that individuals reflect on and participate in the world through the organized evaluation of evidence and argumentation to decide what to believe or do (Ennis, 1987; Jiménez-Aleixandre & Puig, 2012).

Science education has long accepted that critical thinking should be a focus in instruction. The *National Science Education Standards* (see also) advocate the use of inquiry (see also) which demands critical thinking if it is be applied effectively. Inquiry includes components relating to and fostering critical thinking such as 'identification of assumptions, use of critical and logical thinking, and consideration of alternative explanations" (National Academy of Sciences, 1996, p. 23).

There is no single list of features that define critical thinking but Ennis (2011), suggests that ideal critical thinkers:

1. Care that their positions and decisions are justifiable by seeking and being open to alternate hypotheses, explanations, sources, plans, and conclusions; by considering other peoples' points of views and by staying well informed.
2. Ensure that they understand and present all known opinions clearly and honorably by listening to and discovering others views and reasons for those views; by communicating clearly and precisely, by remaining aware of their core beliefs, and by considering the entire situation.
3. Are concerned that others not be confused or intimidated by "their critical thinking prowess" (p. 2) and by reflecting and considering others' level of understanding and feelings.

As an example of critical thinking, consider how high school biology teachers might respond to the question 'Does Smoking Cause Strokes?" Students would have to evaluate the causal link of the claim as well as rely on background knowledge of biology related to strokes and experimental research on the cause of strokes while guarding against leaping to conclusions and considering all alternatives. Their justification will depend on issues such as the rigors and design of the studies and other evidence used to support their argument (Bailin, 2002).

Balin, S. (2002). Critical thinking and science education. *Science & Education, 11*(4), 361-375.
Ennis, R. H. (1987). A taxonomy of critical thinking dispositions and abilities. In J. Baron & R. Sternberg (Eds.), *Teaching thinking skills: Theory and practice* (pp. 9-26). New York: W. H. Freeman.
Ennis, R. H. (2011). The nature of critical thinking: An outline of critical thinking dispositions and abilities. Retrieved from http://faculty.education.illinois.edu/rhennis/documents /TheNatureofCriticalThinking_51711_000.pdf
Jiménez, M. P., & Puig, B. (2012). Argumentation, evidence evaluation, and critical thinking. In B. J. Fraser et al. (Eds.), *Second international handbook of science education* (pp. 1001-1015). Springer International Handbooks of Education.
National Academy of Sciences. (1996). *National Science Education Standards*. Washington, DC: National Academy Press.

Crosscutting Concepts are unifying concepts, ideas, and practices that can be applied across all four domains of science (life sciences, earth and space sciences, physical sciences, and biology). These concepts are common themes that provide a link across the domains and are ones that appear repeatedly in the study of science.

The use of crosscutting concepts in teaching is one of the major recommendations found in the U.S. National Research Council's (2011) *A Framework for K-12 Science Education* (Framework) and Achieve's (2013) *Next Generation Science Standards* (NGSS) (see also) developed from the Framework. This recommendation that science teaching should be based on the use of crosscutting concepts or themes is very similar to that proposed in the *Science Framework for California Public Schools* in 1990. A major difference is that both science and engineering concepts are now included together.

The list of crosscutting concepts linking the fields of science and engineering found in both the Framework (National Research Council, 2011) and the NGSS (Achieve, 2013) are:

1. Patterns
2. Cause and effect: Mechanism and explanation
3. Scale, proportion, and quantity
4. Systems and system models
5. Energy and matter: Flows, cycles, and conservation (called Energy and Matter in Systems in the *Next Generation Science Standards*)
6. Structure and function
7. Stability and change (called Stability and Change in Systems in *Next Generation Science Standards*)

The rationale for the use of crosscutting conceptions in instruction (Achieve, 2013) is that they may be applied to provide an organizing schema on which students might "hang" or place new knowledge. Further, an understanding of these concepts could provide students with a framework for understanding the world through a scientific lens.

The authors of the NGSS have described how each grade band (K-2, 3-5, 6-8, 9-12) will use each of the crosscutting concepts in the classroom and have included a list of performance expectations for each grade band. This should be cross-referenced with the Disciplinary Core Idea Progression document in Appendix E of the standards. For ease of organization and quick viewing, each crosscutting concept is represented in a matrix in Appendix G with the grade band's corresponding crosscutting statement(s). Teachers are asked to integrate each of the dimensions when planning as the crosscutting concepts are not intended to be additional content but rather considered as a structure for teaching the disciplinary core ideas and scientific practices (Achieve, 2013). (AB)

Achieve, Inc. (2013). *The Next Generation Science Standards.* Washington, DC: Author. Retrieved from http://www.nextgenscience.org/three-dimensions

National Research Council. (2011). *A framework for K-12 science education: Practices, crosscutting concepts, and core ideas.* Washington, DC: National Academies Press.

Science Framework for California Public Schools. (1990). Sacramento: California Department of Education.

Culturally Relevant Pedagogy (CRP) is a teaching orientation that references students' culture when teaching to empower "students intellectually, socially, emotionally, and politically" (Ladson-Billings, 1994, 17–18).

CRP draws upon students' background, knowledge, and culture experiences as a source of examples and teaching strategies to help students understand science concepts by connecting students' lives outside and inside of school. Some have recommended including students' preferred modes of learning as part of CRP although this technique is problematic given the lack of empirical support for such a strategy (Pashler et al., 2009).

Based on a study of teachers of students of color, Ladson-Billings (1995) suggests using the following three criteria for CRP. Teachers should focus on the academic needs of their students and foster in them a desire for academic achievement. They should foster cultural competence by allowing students to use their cultural language, dress styles, interaction styles, and take pride in their cultural heritage as part of learning. For instance, some students might find it culturally relevant to write and sing a rap song to help them remember and/or explain complex science processes.

Finally, Ladson-Billings (1995) suggests that teachers help students develop a critical consciousness of the cultural norms and values of society by encouraging questions and debater about the authority of textbooks and other sources of information. In a way related to S/T/S and the use of socio-cultural issues (see also) some CRP plans encourage students to write letters or take other actions to inform others of questionable practices taking place in their communities to try to enact change. For instance, if in a study of biology, students find that the community pond is being polluted by runoff from a nearby farm; students may contact the owners and request measures to prevent this practice.

CRP recognizes the place of cultural practices as a part of learning science. Although it is not prescriptive, it should be viewed as a way to reduce the disparities between students in increasingly diverse classrooms (Patchen & Cox-Peterson, 2008). It is important that the cultural information added to the class should be important and relevant. Montellano (1997) cautions against adding culturally related information that lacks scientific importance in an attempt to reach certain students. Rather, he says that science instruction must be standards-based but include obvious culturally relevant examples. (PW)

Ladson-Billings, G. (1994). *The dreamkeepers: Successful teachers of African-American children.* San Francisco: Jossey-Bass.

Ladson-Billings, G. (1995). But that's just good teaching! The case for culturally relevant pedagogy. *Theory into Practice, 35*(3), 159-165.

Montellano, B. O. (1997). Teaching multicultural science rigorously: Culturally relevant science. Retrieved from: http://www.academia.edu/870305/Teaching_Multicultural_Science_Rigorously_Culturally_Relevant_Science

Pashler, H., McDaniel, M., Rohrer, D., & Bjork, R. (2009). Learning styles: Concepts and evidence. *Psychological Science in the Public Interest, 9*(3), 105-119.

Patchen, T., & Cox-Peterson, A. (2008). Constructing cultural relevance in science: A case study of two elementary teachers. *Science Education, 92*(6), 994-1014.

Curriculum typically is the list of courses in an educational institution (such as in a secondary school) or the content included in a particular school subject (such as biology).

Curriculum comes from *currere* or Latin for "the course to be run," originally associated with ancient chariot races but more recently signifies the sequence of courses or other learning experiences provided in schools. So, the word curriculum may simply be "a plan for learning" (Taba, 1962, p.11) often linked to a particular school subject such as high school chemistry. Or, it might represent all of the learning experiences, planned and unplanned, that occur in a particular educational institution (Marsh & Willis, 2003). Regardless of how it is defined, Null (2011) says, "Curriculum is the heart of education" (p.11) because it describes what should be taught by combining thought, action, and purpose.

A description of the curriculum for a particular subject might include both content goals and instructional methods. For instance, the curriculum for secondary school biology might feature topics such as cell anatomy, genetics, and classification, and it might specify that the class should be taught using a project-based (see also) or inquiry methods (see also). This description might be provided in a document from many sources such as a department or ministry of education or the school itself. It might also be implied by the textbook or come from the teacher. In many instances, the ultimate curriculum that students experience in the classroom is very likely inspired by many sources.

In addition to the traditional definition, many scholars also recognize different forms of the curriculum including the "ideal" curriculum, the "intended" curriculum and the "received" curriculum, and several other forms. For instance, the "ideal" curriculum is what experts in the field recommend. The "intended" curriculum is what the teacher planned to teach, and the "received" curriculum is what students actually take away from a lesson and from the course.

True curricular knowledge also includes having information about the "vertical" curriculum in a particular subject by knowing what students have learned in previous years and knowing that they are expected to learn in the future. Knowing which materials and programs are available and relevant to teaching specific domains of science and even specific topics within that domain are another essential component of science curricular knowledge (Gess-Newsome & Lederman, 1999). (PW)

Gess-Newsome, J., & Lederman, N.G. (1999). *Examining pedagogical content knowledge: The construct and its implications for Science Education*. Boston, MA: Kluwer Academic.
Marsh, C. J., & Willis, G. (2003). *Curriculum: Alternative approaches, ongoing issues* (3rd ed.). Upper Saddle River, NJ: Merrill Prentice Hall.
Null, W. (2011). *Curriculum: From theory to practice*. New York, NY: Rowman & Littlefield Publishers, Inc.
Taba, H. (1962). *Curriculum development: Theory and practice*. New York: Harcourt, Brace and World, Inc.

Deduction (Deductive Thinking) is a type of reasoning (see also) used to test and evaluate scientific ideas while induction (see also) is the process used to form the ideas and generalizations. For instance, if we have a law that all objects fall toward the ground at the same rate no matter how heavy they are, we could test this by dropping many pairs of light and heavy objects and measuring their speed. This test is called deduction or hypothetico-deductivism (see also) (McComas, 2004).

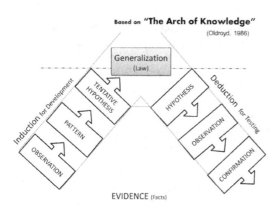

Oldroyd (1986) describes the method of science and the relationship between induction and deduction as 'the arch of knowledge.' The arch begins with the use of induction (see also) to form patterns, generalizations or laws (see also) from those observations. The best generalizations are those that contain and account for the most observations but no generalization can be proven; they can only be shown to be false. We may continually show that all pairs of heavy and light objects fall toward the ground with the same speed, but this does not prove the generalization because some future observation may not follow this pattern. Of course, this is highly unlikely but must be considered a possibility.

Many scientific ideas are tested using the hypothetico-deductive (H/D) method, which is the other vital aspect of the "arch of knowledge." H/D begins with the proposal of a hypothesis that can be tested. In the case of our example of falling objects, one might propose that a ball made from a new kind of metal might fall faster than a ball of steel. The second step includes conducting an experiment or gathering observations to test the hypothesis. If the two balls fall at the same speed, the generalization is supported, but still not proved since that is impossible in science.

The roles of induction and deduction are central to the nature of science (see also) but the science education literature typically focuses on induction as a knowledge generating tool while deduction is rarely mentioned. Students should be given opportunities to use both types of reasoning as they explore the "arch of knowledge." (Oldroyd, 1986) (CB)

McComas, W. F. (2004). Keys to teaching the nature of science: Focusing on the nature of science in the science classroom. *The Science Teacher, 71*(9), 24-27.

Oldroyd, D. R. (1986). *The arch of knowledge: An introductory study of the history of the philosophy and methodology of science.* New York, NY: Methuen.

Diagnostic Assessments are pre-assessments that provide instructors information about learners' prior knowledge, understandings, and misconceptions before introduction of a new concept or activity. The diagnostic assessment may also be used to set a baseline for how much academic growth has occurred by the time the lesson is complete. Just as in medical practice, the true purpose of diagnostic assessment is to identify learning challenges so that students can be given appropriate "treatments."

Kellough et al. (1999) lists seven purposes for assessment and all of these may be useful to diagnose (and report) students' learning challenges and needs:

1. Identify students' strengths and weaknesses
2. Assist students in learning by pointing out their strengths and weaknesses
3. Assess and improve teacher effectiveness
4. Assess the effectiveness of a specific instructional strategy
5. Assess and improve the effectiveness of the science curriculum
6. Provide data for decision making purposes (such as awarding grades)
7. Communicate with parents

There are four main types of assessments including formative (see also), summative (see also), authentic (assessments reflecting real-world applications that are aligned with curriculum objectives), and the diagnostic form discussed here.

Some assessment experts consider diagnostic assessments to be a type of formative assessment; most agree that it is a unique and distinct form (McMillan et al., 2000). In some situations where the lessons are continuous, such as in a unit on genetics, the **summative** assessment for the lesson on *probability and heredity* could serve as a **diagnostic** assessment for the next lesson on *meiosis and Punnett squares.*

Science teachers could use a diagnostic assessment at the very beginning of the year to check for any misconceptions or issues students might have in order to provide appropriate lessons for those who need it. In this case, the diagnostic assessment is given for the purpose of measuring students' learning needs, not for providing a grade.

In conclusion, any assessment can be used diagnostically regardless of when the assessment is conducted (pre-instruction, during instruction, or post-instruction). At any time, any information about student performance can inform teachers about the progress, knowledge, understanding, and misconceptions of the class, a subgroup of students, or an individual student. (AR)

Kellough, R. D., Kellough, N. G., & Kim, E. C. (1999). *Secondary school teaching: A guide to methods and resources.* Upper Saddle River, NJ: Merrill, Inc.

McMillan, J. H., Hellsten, L., Kelly, I. W., Noonan, B., & Klinger, D. (2000). *Classroom assessment: Principles and practice for effective instruction.* Toronto, CA: Pearson.

Didactic Instruction (Greek didaktikos, *apt to teach, taught,* didak-, *to teach, educate)* is also called direct instruction or explicit teaching. In short, didactic teaching consists of the teacher transmitting information directly to the students in the most explicit way possible.

Didactic instruction may involve lecture presentations, modeling, demon-strations and explanations interspersed with checks for student understanding and teacher-monitored practice. Such a model of teaching is viewed as teacher-centered (as opposed to student-centered) as the teacher selects and directs the learning tasks and remains the central focus during instruction while the student is viewed as the recipient of information (Joyce et al., 2008).

Sometimes didactic instruction is considered negatively as a mode of instruction particularly when this instruction is portrayed as little more than the teacher talking while students sit passively in their desks along with the hope that they are learning something. Critics of this kind of teaching cite the short attention spans of students which might make it difficult for them to stay focused and engaged on the teacher if this is the only form of instruction used (Kinder & Carnine, 1991).

The classic use of didactic instruction is actually quite positive. Used properly, its goal of developing direct communications with students without regard to content, basic skills, or higher order thinking skills can be achieved. In fact, many studies reveal that direct instruction or didactic teaching may make positive impacts on educational gains especially among certain sub-populations of students, for example, low-income and special education students (Kinder & Carnine, 1991). Didactic teaching, however, is not typically helpful for teaching complex processes, critical thinking skills, problem solving or teaching students to think creatively (Woolfolk, 2013); inquiry and other discovery modes are preferred.

It is best to consider didactic instruction in terms of the skills and passion with which it is used, the goals held by the instructor and the classroom context in which it is applied. According to Woolfolk, (2013), didactic instruction is best utilized to teach unambiguous information such as science facts, vocabulary, computation, and step-by-step procedures. Every subject likely requires the use of some didactic instruction, thus the technique itself should not be viewed negatively or positively, it is simply a tool in the suite of skills good teachers possess. (PW)

Kinder, D., & Carnine, D. (1991). Direct instruction: What is it, and what is it becoming? *Journal of Behavioral Education, 1*(2), 193-213.

Joyce, B. R., Weil, M., & Calhoun, E. (2008). *Models of teaching* (8th ed.). Boston, MA: Pearson/Allyn and Bacon Publishers.

Woolfolk, A. (2013). *Educational psychology* (12th ed.). Boston, MA: Pearson.

Differentiation (Differentiated Instruction) is an instructional philosophy and accompanying methodology in which teachers provide extra support for some students and extra challenges for those students for whom enrichment might result in deeper learning. Differentiating teachers acknowledge that despite fundamental similarities among learners, these same learners are individuals with academic, cultural, and experiential differences (Allan and Tomlinson & McTighe, 2000; Nunley, 2006).

Differentiating compels teachers to discover the academic starting places of students as well as students' experiences with and interest in the content through formative assessments. Throughout the unit teachers use what they have learned through formative assessment to differentiate using flexible approaches to curriculum, instruction, grouping, timing, and assessment. In each case the teacher focuses on the essentials of the subject in her planning and instruction. The teacher provides choices to students and highlights the growth of the individual student. Differentiation is an example of responsive, inclusive, and equitable instruction in that it takes into account the individual's needs rather than providing exactly the same learning experience for all students.

In a science classroom, differentiation might entail distributing readings on the same topic but of varying lengths and difficulties to specific students or groups of students based on what the teacher knows about the students' reading readiness. In summary, teachers can differentiate content, process, and products, although teachers may not be able to differentiate for all students all of the time.

An example of differentiation in the science classroom may be found in Tomlinson (1999).

> Mrs. Santos often assigns students in her class to reading squads when they work with text materials. At this stage, group assignments usually are made so students of similar reading levels work together. She varies graphic organizers and learning log prompts according to the amount of structure and concreteness the various groups need to grasp essential understandings from the chapter. She also makes it possible for students to read aloud in their groups or to read silently. Then they complete organizers and prompts together. As students read, Mrs. Santos moves among groups. Sometimes she reads key passages to them, sometimes she asks them to read to her, but she always probes for deeper understanding and helps to clarify their thinking. (p. 5) (AB)

Allan, S. D., & Tomlinson, C. A. (2000). *Leadership for differentiating schools and classrooms*. Alexandria, VA: Association for Supervision and Curriculum Development.

Nunley, K. (2006). *Differentiating the high school classroom: Solution strategies for 18 common obstacles*. Thousand Oaks, CA: Corbin Press.

Tomlinson, C. A. (1999). *The differentiated classroom: Responding to the needs of all learners*. Alexandria, VA: Association for Supervision and Curriculum Development.

Tomlinson, C. A., & McTighe, J. (2000). *Integrating differentiated instruction and understanding by design: Connecting content and kids*. Alexandria, VA: Association for Supervision and Curriculum Development.

Discovery Learning (Teaching) is a type of inquiry-based, constructivist teaching (see also) in which students investigate problems presented by the teacher or selected from personal interests (Moore, 2009) to look at examples and phenomena in the natural world, reach personal conclusions, and construct personal understanding of the process. It is a kind of "learning by doing" with varying levels of teacher involvement.

The psychologist Jerome Bruner proposed discovery teaching in the middle of the 20th century by suggesting that knowing is a process distinct from simply accumulating the wisdom of science in textbooks. He suggested that all learners are problem solvers who interact with the natural world to test ideas and propose patterns through personal discovery (Hassard & Dias, 2009).

Discovery learning is one of several modes of inquiry (see also) teaching. (Edelson et al., 1999). While inquiry is also a specific kind of problem solving (see also), there is no established pattern of investigation. Discovery learning follows the methods of science where students are exposed to questions and experiences in such a way that they "discover" for themselves the intended concepts. Such problem solving is "guided" by teachers to some degree because there is no expectation that students would naturally arrive at ideas identical to those of scientists (Hammer, 1997).

Discovery learning can be used several ways depending on the level of involvement of the teacher (Moore, 2009). At each increasing level, learning becomes more student-centered. At the open level, students engage in their own scientific study, make their own investigations and observations and develop, articulate, and defend their own explanations.

- Level I (Guided discovery). The problem and processes for solving the problem are provided by the teacher;
- Level II (Modified discovery). The problem is generated by the teacher but the processes for solving the problem and the solutions to the problem are determined by the students; and
- Level III (Open discovery). Students generate the problem, decide on the processes for solving the problem, and provide the solution.

Moore (2009) noted that active learning results in a higher degree of intrinsic motivation in students. Learners construct their own knowledge and, therefore, have a stake in the ownership of that knowledge. Most discovery learning requires that students work cooperatively to encourage social skill development. (LW)

Edelson, D., Gordin, D. N., & Pea, R. D. (1999). Addressing the challenges of inquiry-based learning through technology and curriculum design. *The Journal of Learning Sciences, 8*(3/4), 391-450.

Hammer, D. (1997). Discovery learning and discovery teaching. *Cognition and Instruction, 15*(4), 485- 529.

Hassard, J., & Dias, M. (2009). *The art of teaching science.* New York, NY: Routledge.

Moore, K. (2009). *Effective instructional strategies.* Thousand Oaks, CA: Sage Publications, Inc.

Discrepant Events (Puzzling Phenomena) are phenomena, puzzles, questions or other learning experiences presented by the teacher to students that appear to contradict the laws of nature or what students expect to occur, thus causing students to wonder why a particular event or phenomenon occurred.

Discrepant events or puzzling phenomena are student-specific but occur when students' experience cognitive dissonance as their predictions of what should happen do not match the reality of what actually occurs. Thus, such events can be used as effective motivational tools to prompt students to want to know more about the subject in order to explain the event.

Consider the following examples of discrepant events (Friedl, 1986):

- What happens when a small cork is floated in the middle of a partly-filled glass of water? (The cork always floats to the side of the glass.)
- When happens to the total volume when 50 mls of alcohol are added to 50 mls of water in a graduated cylinder? (The total is *not* 100mls.)
- Pour about an inch of water in a bucket and swing the bucket overhead in a large upright circle. (The water stays in the bucket.)

These events can prompt deep learning and meaning-making on the part of the student if used expertly by the teacher.

Some science teachers choose to use discrepant events for a single science lesson, while others employ the strategy throughout a unit, having students continually work toward answering why that event occurred. When faced with these events, students often have difficulty giving up their original ideas about science. They may not immediately abandon or alter their pre-instructional ideas, and this obstacle calls for educators to be prepared with strategies to address this issue. Also, science teachers should be careful to not just use discrepant events to amaze students and leave the event unexplained (Wright & Govindarajan, 1995) and bypass the science content learning that could occur as a result of a structured cycle of learning (see learning cycle).

One such cycle, a three-step model developed by Friedl (1986), leads students through a meaning-making process to help resolve any cognitive dissonance students might experience and addresses students' reluctance to give up pre-instructional misconceptions: 1) Set up the discrepant event, 2) Involve the students in solving the discrepancy, and 3) Resolve the questions posed by the events and relate them to a body of science knowledge. The role of the instructor in following up with students' ideas in each step of this cycle is critical to the deep learning science educators aim for in their instruction. (AB)

Friedl, A. E. (1986). *Teaching science to children: An integrated approach.* New York: Random House

Wright, E. L., & Govindarajan, G. (1995). *The Science Teacher, 62*(1), 25-28.

Disciplinary Core Ideas are the concepts deemed to be the most important for students to learn and for teachers to teach and assess in science.

Disciplinary Core ideas comprise the third dimension in the National Research Council's (NRC) *A Framework for K-12 Science Education* which provides the basis for the *Next Generation Science Standards* (NGSS). According to the authors of the NGSS, for an idea to be considered "core," it must meet from two to four of the following criteria:

- Have broad importance across multiple sciences or engineering disciplines or be a key organizing concept of a single discipline;
- Provide a key tool for understanding or investigating more complex ideas and solving problems;
- Relate to the interests and life experiences of students or be connected to societal or personal concerns that require scientific or technological knowledge;
- Be teachable and learnable over multiple grades at increasing levels of depth and sophistication.

The core ideas in the NGSS are grouped in four domains: Life Sciences, Earth and Space Sciences, Physical Sciences, and Engineering, Technology, and Applications of Science. The core ideas within each domain are typically the big ideas that students must understand to have a foundational understanding of that domain. The disciplinary core ideas in the physical sciences, for example, include:

1. Matter and its Interactions
2. Motion and Stability: Forces and Interactions
3. Energy
4. Waves and their applications in technologies for information transfer

Each core idea has sub-ideas or component ideas listed below it, and the framework also includes an essential question for each core and component idea in its elaboration of these ideas.

The disciplinary core ideas are to be taught in conjunction with the other two dimensions, which are the scientific and engineering practices (See also) (Dimension 1) and the crosscutting concepts (See also) (Dimension 2). By teaching core ideas along with practices, teachers are able to add content to otherwise dry processes, and by layering on the crosscutting concepts, teachers provide an organizational scheme to which students can relate the core ideas from across the domains (Achieve, 2013). (AB)

Achieve, Inc. (2013). *The next generation science standards*. Washington, DC: Author. Retrieved from http://www.nextgenscience.org/three-dimensions.
National Research Council (U.S.). (2011). *A framework for K-12 science education: Practices, crosscutting concepts, and core ideas*. Washington, DC: National Academies Press.

Environmental Education (EE) is an instructional approach designed to develop citizens who are environmentally literate and have knowledge and understanding of the biophysical environment and its associated problems, are *aware* of how to help solve these problems by applying basic ecological concepts, and *motivated* to work toward solutions to environmental problems or issues (Stapp et al., 1998; David, 1974; Roth, 1992).

EE has a long history and incorporates aspects of nature study, conservation education, and outdoor education (Disinger, 1985) (see also). EE traces its foundation in two important documents, *The Belgrade Charter* published in 1975 and *Tbilisi Declaration* published in 1977.

The *Belgrade Charter* proposed a global framework for environmental education, one that develops citizens who are aware of and concerned about the environment and its associated problems, but who also possess the knowledge, skills, attitudes, motivations, and commitment to work individually and collectively toward solutions of current problems and the prevention of new ones.

The *Tiblisi Declaration* expanded on the *Charter* by citing specific overarching goals for EE which serve as the foundation of EE today. These include (a) fostering clear awareness of, and concern about economic, social, political, and ecological interdependence in urban and rural settings; (b) providing every person with opportunities to acquire knowledge, values, attitudes, commitment and skills needed to protect and improve the environment; and (c) creating new patterns of behavior of individuals, groups and society as a whole towards the environment. (UNESCO, 1978, pp. 26-27).

According to the Tiblisi Declaration, EE has an additional five primary instructional goals including:

- Developing awareness and sensitivity to the environment and environmental problems;
- Building knowledge and understanding of the environment and environmental problems;
- Fostering attitudes of concern for the environment;
- Developing skills to identify and solve environmental problems; and
- Encouraging participation for active involvement in solving environmental problems (UNESCO, 1978). (CW)

David, T. G. (1974). Environmental literacy. *The School Review, 82*(4), 687-705.

Disinger, J. F. (1985). What research says. *School Science and Mathematics, 85*(1), 59-68.

Roth, C. E. (1992). *Environmental literacy: Its roots, evolution, and direction in the 1990s.* Washington, DC: Office of Educational Research and Improvement.

Stapp, W. B., Bennett, D., Bryan Jr., W., Fulton, J., MacGregor, J., & Nowark, P. (1998). The concept of environmental education. In H. R. Hungerford, W. J. Bluhm, T. L. Volk, & J. M. Ramsey (Eds.), *Essential readings in environmental education* (pp. 33-36). Champaign, IL: Stipes Publishing.

UNESCO. (1978). *Final report, Intergovernmental Conference on Environmental Education,* organized by UNESCO in cooperation with UNEP, Tbilisi, USSR. Paris: Author.

Ethics in Science may refer to appropriate standards in conducting research or to moral/ethical proper standards regarding the use of scientific information in society.

Students should be exposed to both kinds of ethics in the science classroom. First, students should be made aware of the way in which scientists should engage in scientific work as they investigate the natural world. Resnik (2005) identified twelve such principles including: honesty, carefulness, openness, freedom, credit, education, social responsibility, legality, opportunity, mutual respect, efficiency, and respect for others. These might be called professional scientific ethics and apply to people who occupy a professional occupation role (Bayles, 1988). Scientists are members of a profession, and as such, should follow established professional standards (Shrader-Frechette, 1994).

Second, students should be made aware of the notion that the ethical conduct in science should not violate accepted moral standards generally in conduct of or as a result of scientific work.

Resnick (2005) points out that scientists have been linked to secret testing on human beings during WWII, issues associated with the Human Genome Project, the cloning of human embryos and animals, and debates about global climate change. Finally, because science has become intertwined with business and industry, there is a perceived potential ethical conflict between scientific values and business or economic values (Reiser, 1993). (LW)

Bayles. M. (1988). *Professional ethics* (2nd ed.). Belmont, CA: Wadsworth.

Reiser, S. (1993). The ethics movement in the biological sciences: A new voyage of discovery. In R. Bulger, E. Heitman, & S. Reiser (Eds.), *The ethical dimensions of biological sciences.* New York, NY: Cambridge University Press.

Resnik, D. B. (2005). *The ethics of science.* New York, NY: Routledge.

Shrader-Frechette, K. (1994). *Ethics of scientific research.* Boston, MA: Rowman and Littlefield.

Experiential Learning (also referred to as experience-based learning) is an instructional approach in which students learn through direct experience and reflection. These experiences can be either spontaneous or designed and orchestrated by the teacher for specific instructional purposes.

David A. Kolb (1984) popularized the idea of experiential learning (EL) with the Experiential Learning Model (ELM) developed from the work of Jean Piaget, John Dewey and Kurt Lewin. In ELM, which has many characteristics of a learning cycle (See also) the learner engages a four stage cycle that includes having (1) concrete experiences ("DO"), (2) observation and reflection ("OBSERVE"), (3) forming abstract concepts ("THINK"), and (4) testing ideas in new situations ("PLAN").

The learner must also (a) be a willing and active participant in the experience; (b) reflect on the experience; (c) possess and use analytical skills to conceptualize the experience; and (d) possess decision making and problem solving skills in order to use the new ideas gained from the experience (Itin, 1999).

EL is not discipline-specific and can be utilized to teach various concepts, skills, issues, and relationships in which the learner develops understanding and knowledge based on firsthand experience, rather than only from more traditional approaches EL can incorporate aspects of adventure learning, service learning, free choice learning, cooperative learning, and internships.

EL requires that learners investigate a question that ideally students would perceive as relevant (although they may not sense the relevance immediately), supported by activities that provide worthwhile experiences that engage the learner in seeking answers to the question. There must also be an intention to learn, active participation in the experience, and focus on the individual's learning processes that incorporates both the particular experience and reflection on that experience.

In experiential learning, as with other non-traditional approaches, the teacher is a facilitator, providing only enough guidance to help students to succeed or assisting them to see connections among concepts and activities (Adkins & Simmons, 2002; Chapman et al., 1992) and supported by reflection, critical analysis, and synthesis on the part of the student in order to deepen the learning experience.

In the best examples of EL, learners become emotionally engaged and immersed in the learning and may see themselves as part of the learning experience (Adkins & Simmons, 2002). (CW)

Adkins, C., & Simmons, B. (2002). Outdoor, experiential, and environmental education: Converging or diverging approaches? Charleston, WV: ERIC/CRESS. Retrieved from http://www.eric.ed.gov/PDFS/ED467713.pdf

Chapman, S., McPhee, P., & Proudman, B. (1992). What is experiential education? *The Journal of Experiential Education, 15*(2), 101-108.

Itin, C. M. (1999). Reasserting the philosophy of experiential education as a vehicle for change in the 21st century. *The Journal of Experiential Education, 22*(2), 91-98.

Kolb, D. (1984). *Experiential learning as the science of learning and development.* Englewood Cliffs, NJ: Prentice Hall.

Framework for K-12 Science Education, published in July 2011 by the U.S. National Research Council (NRC) of the National Academy of Sciences, is the foundation for the development of the *Next Generation Science Standards*. The *Framework* uses the latest scientific, cognitive, and educational research as its basis for identifying the science content, skills, and practices that all K-12 students should know.

The *Framework* was developed by eighteen individuals who are well-known in their fields as well as four design teams that represent the four domains of science (life science, physical science, earth and space science, and engineering). The perceived need by the science and/or science education communities for new science standards, as well as a framework to undergird these new standards, stemmed from multiple reasons. First, the move to Common Core (CCSSO, 2010) (sell also) standards for mathematics and English/Language Arts signaled an opportunity for the science community to move toward new science standards. Although there are existing science standards, they were developed in the mid-1990s, and new science developments as well as new research in teaching and learning have been released since that time.

Another rationale for a more comprehensive set of standards is the push to create students who are more informed citizens and have a better understanding of issues that impact us on a local, national, and global level, as well as citizens who are better able to compete in the global market. Educators should aim to mold students who are careful consumers of information, and who can enter their careers of choice, especially careers in science and engineering.

However, before developing these new standards a framework had to be created so that there were unifying aspects underlying the standards. Therefore, the *Framework* is based on three dimensions around which standards and instruction should be built: crosscutting concepts, disciplinary core ideas, and science and engineering practices. These three dimensions lay out a set of integrated expectations for science and engineering in grades K-12 (NRC, 2011).

Science teachers can use the *Framework* as a preview of the Next Generation Science Standards to revise curriculum, instruction, and assessment. The Framework offers background information on how the standards were developed and more in-depth information about how to navigate the three dimensions of the *Framework*. (AB)

Council of Chief State School Officers. (2010). *Common core state standards initiative.* Washington, DC: Author. Retrieved from http://www.corestandards.org/
National Research Council. (2011). *A framework for K-12 science education: Practices, crosscutting concepts, and core ideas.* Washington, DC: National Academies Press.

For more information and to supplement understanding of this entry please see: Next Generation Science Standards, Disciplinary Core Ideas, Crosscutting Concepts, and Scientific and Engineering Practices.

Frameworks (General Definition) contain a description of the learning goals that should be achieved by students in an educational system, typically in a particular discipline (such as science). Frameworks generally include a list of content standards indicating what should be taught in schools, a review of the research behind the development of the standards, guiding principles, and other visionary aspects of the goals desired for all students to achieve.

Frameworks documents, also called curriculum frameworks, provide a broad description of the content and the sequence of learning expected of all students by the time they graduate from high school. Framework development is the first step toward developing clear and high quality standards that all students are expected to achieve. Frameworks suggest the best thinking about what students should know, understand, and be able to do within a particular discipline (Curry & Temple, 1992). By providing a structure for the curricular components of the instructional system, frameworks are used to guide curriculum development in both formal and informal settings (National Research Council, 2012) by suggesting resources and appropriate models for curriculum developers to use (Parkay et al., 2010). Frameworks may also include recommendations or requirements about *how* a particular subject should be taught such as the use of inquiry in the teaching of science.

The framework document is usually developed at a regional or national level as a collaborative effort among educators representing different facets of society which would include educators, politicians, industry representatives, educational researchers and members of the public. A framework is designed to bring standards and classroom practice together. They provide guidance for the organization of specific knowledge and instruction and can help facilitate policy decisions at the school level (Curry & Temple, 1992). In the U.S. where education is largely governed at the level of the individual states, developing a new framework every six or seven years is typical so that the goals of education can remain relevant and current. (PW)

Curry, B., & Temple, T. (1992). *Using curriculum frameworks for systemic reform.* Alexandria, VA: Association for Supervision and Curriculum Development.

National Research Council. (2012). *A framework for K-12 science education: Practices, crosscutting concepts, and core ideas.* Committee on a Conceptual Framework for New K-12 Science Education Standards. Board on Science Education, Division of Behavioral and Social Sciences and Education. Washington, DC: The National Academies Press.

Parkay, F., Anctil, E. J., & Hass, G. (2010). *Curriculum leadership: Readings for developing quality educational programs* (9th ed.). Boston, MA: Allyn & Bacon.

Formative Assessment refers not to the type of student evaluation, but to the timing of that evaluation. Formative, unlike summative, occurs during instruction and, therefore, has a different purpose than assessment that takes place after the learning activity has occurred (as is the case with summative assessment (See also).

According to Yorke (2003) and Black and Wiliam (1998) formative assessment occurs during instruction in order to provide feedback while the student takes part in the learning activity rather than at the end of the learning activity. This can provide feedback to students about their current performance so they might make changes in their study techniques or seek additional help that will positively impact their academic achievement. Learning about student performance while instruction is still occurring will also help teachers make useful changes in instruction that could assist students learning the current material. Summative assessment, another type of assessment, occurs at the end of instruction so there is no opportunity to assist the current group of students.

Formative assessment has three main elements (Rushton, 2005). First, formative assessment is an important way to enable learning and in particular deep learning. Second, feedback is the central component of effective formative assessment. Finally, the use of formative assessment may help to change our existing assessment philosophy that places too much emphasis on summative assessment.

According to Cowie and Bell (1999) there are two types of formative assessment; planned and interactive. The planned formative assessment involves obtaining feedback from the whole class about progress made toward reaching the learning goals. It is called *planning formative assessment* because teachers consciously develop and implement the activities necessary to assess their students. *Interactive formative assessment* occurs during individual student-teacher interactions. It is based on the ability of the teachers to notice their students' actions and respond instantaneously. Whether planned or interactive, formative assessment provides teachers and students with valuable information that can be used to adjust the curriculum and to assist students in learning the material successfully. (AR)

Black, P., & Wiliam, D. (1998). Assessment and classroom learning. *Assessment in Education*, 5(1), 7-74.

Cowie, B., & Bell, B. (1999). A model of formative assessment in science education. *Assessment in Education*, 6(1), 101-116.

Rushton, A. (2005). Formative assessment: A key to deep learning? *Medical Teacher*, 27(6), 509-513.

Yorke, M. (2003). Formative assessment in higher education: moves towards theory and the enhancement of pedagogic practice. *Higher Education*, 45(4), 477-501.

Globalization of Science Education is the increasing interest shown by many nations in promoting science instruction in schools with shared goals, methods, modes of assessment, and scholarly contributions from diverse communities across the world.

Globalization has occurred rapidly in recent years because of the ease of sharing ideas and collaborating with others due to modern communications technology. Ideas and concerns about science teaching and learning have become highly internationalized increasingly making science education a global pursuit. At least three major indicators of globalization are evident in science education including shared instructional programs, cross-national assessment of educational progress, and an increase in contributions to research and development in science teaching from scholars worldwide.

Sharing of ideas has resulted in increasingly shared goals for science teaching and learning as reflected in standards documents from diverse nations. There are cross national programs such as the International Baccalaureate (IB) degree programs, increasing unification of higher education in Europe as suggested by the Bologna agreement and common practices related to science teacher preparation (Charlton & Andras, 2006).

Another component of globalization in science education relates to sharing information through global data collection projects. An example of this is the *Globe Program* which features an environmental curriculum, and students participate in similar hands-on activities around the world and share the collected data (see S/T/S, socio-scientific problems and authentic science education).

We see globalization in the international studies comparing student achievement and instructional methods. Major initiatives in this area include the *Trends in International Mathematics and Science Study* (TIMMS), a comparative study of the science and mathematics achievement of fourth and eighth graders show how students compare globally at these grade levels. The *Programme of International Student Achievement* (PISA) was conducted to determine how well high school students were equipped for their role in society by assessing how students apply knowledge in everyday situations. Studies such as these have had a significant impact on the globalization of science education (Fensham, 2011).

Finally, a satisfying trend to globalize science education has occurred through shared research contributions. In the past few decades there has been a dramatic increase in the number of nations represented at science education research conferences and in the research literature itself. (KM)

Charlton, B. G., & Andras, P. (2006). Globalization in science education: An inevitable and beneficial trend. *Medical Hypotheses*, *66*(5), 869-873.

Fensham, P. J. (2011). Globalization of science education: Comment and a commentary. *Journal of Research in Science Teaching*, *48*(6), 698-709.

Hands-on Science refers to instructional activities that give students the opportunity to directly explore, investigate, and/or observe, probe or manipulate objects or scientific phenomena. There are so many permutations and applications of this term that it has little shared meaning, but most agree that it is a form of laboratory (see also) experience.

At its most basic level, the term "hands-on science" simply means that the student is doing something, perhaps manipulating something rather than just passively hearing or reading about science. The range of activities and practices that could be called hands-on is vast resulting in a continuum of activities. At one extreme a young child might be asked to color a drawing of a flower or make a model of a plant. At the other end of the spectrum, a student might work with a professor to use gene sequencing technology to determine if a recently discovered flower is a new species.

Since the students are both using their senses (and their hands) to engage in the work, these activities could be called hands-on. However, it should be very clear that each of these examples requires vastly different skills and would make quite distinct impacts on student learning and attitudes toward science. It is clear that there is a continuum of potential impact in many learning experiences and "hands-on" is no exception. Many educators now prefer the phrase "hands-on/minds-on" because it more accurately conveys the desired characteristics of the activities rather than simply referring to the act of manipulation of objects. If the work to be done in science class is a simple dry lab (see also) or "cut and paste" or "paper and pencil" activity, many would agree that it would very likely not make a huge impact on learning and hence is not "minds on." So, given the lack of a precise definition, much care should be used when an activity is described as hands-on.

Gregory (2002) mentions the powerful role of hands-on experiences in museums and science centers and provides some implications for the use of this technique in schools. He reminds us that the hands-on experience is both personal and necessary and that "individual perception and understanding, require interactive experience with objects (including working models that can be constructed and handled) to approach and appreciate abstract theoretical principles" (p. 184). However, students may learn the wrong lessons if the exploration is completely unguided; teachers must note what students are learning.

Most would agree with Gregory that we need better research regarding the role of hands-on experiences in the classroom. He suggests that we might look at students' reactions when their predictions turn out to be incorrect or to explore students' ability to propose links between different kinds of phenomena and even to investigate students' thinking when nothing seems to have happened as a result of the hands-on investigation. Those who support high quality hands-on investigations would agree with Gregory that hands-on science is an opportunity for "shaking hands with the Universe" (p. 192). (WM)

Gregory, R. L. (2002). Hands-on science in *The challenges for science: Education for the twenty first century*. Pontificia Academia Scientirum Scripta Varia 104. Vatican City: Pontificia Academia Scientirum.

Hypothesis is one of the most frequently used terms in science teaching and usually means "an educated guess" or even just a simple "guess" but the reality is more complex.

As frequently used, in classrooms and professional science settings, the word "hypothesis" has at least three meanings. Using the term one way when others hear it another way could cause problems, thus it is important to appreciate these distinctions and use the term very carefully, if at all.

Prediction; for many teachers, the term "hypothesis" simply means a prediction (a type of guess) about what is going to occur in a laboratory experiment or other investigation. Students are often asked to write their "hypothesis" before doing laboratory work. If the students do not have a clear view of the scientific principles, their hypotheses or predictions may be little more than guesses. Asking students to make hypotheses of this type can be misleading if students come to believe that scientists also make uninformed guesses as they engage in their work.

Trial Theory or Explanatory Hypothesis; if the hypothesis relates to an idea that may become a theory with more evidence and agreement from scientists, it would be best to call this an explanatory hypothesis. In other words, the trial idea (or hypothesis) is not yet validated, but if it is, it would be a scientific theory (Sonleitner, 1989).

Trial Law or Generalizing Hypothesis; if the hypothesis relates to an idea that may become a law with more evidence and agreement from scientists, it would be best to call this a generalizing hypothesis. In other words, the trial idea (or hypothesis) is not yet validated but if it is, it would be a scientific law (Sonleitner, 1989).

Refer to the illustration to visualize the relationship of the three ways that the term "hypothesis" may be used (prediction, generalizing hypothesis and explanatory hypothesis). The definitions of law and theory are themselves quite sophisticated and are defined in detail elsewhere in this glossary and in McComas 2003, 2004). (WM)

McComas, W. F. (2003). A textbook case: Laws and theories in biology instruction. *International Journal of Science and Mathematics Education, 1*(2), 1-15.

McComas, W. F. (2004). Keys to teaching the nature of science: Focusing on the nature of science in the science classroom. *The Science Teacher, 71*(9), 24-27.

Sonleitner, F. J. (1989). Theories, laws and all that. National Center for Science Education. *Newsletter, 9*(6), 4.

Hypothetico-Deduction is a type of reasoning commonly used in science based on a logical pattern which includes idea formation often using induction (See also) and subsequent testing with deductive means. Some suggest that this is *the* method of science.

Hypothetico-deduction (or hypothetico-deductive reasoning) is a dominant logical process within the sciences based on what Oldroyd (1986) has called the "arch of knowledge." Through induction (see also) evidence from observations and/or experiments is collected to the point where a scientist proposes a general-ization worthy of testing. The test takes the form of a predictive hypothesis (see also) which is then evaluated by using the process of deduction (see also).

As an example, consider the entomologist who has collected many examples of a new type of beetle from a particular tropical forest. She finds that the males of that species are reddish in color and the females are dark brown. This is the proposed generalization (or law) based on the available evidence and developed using inductive reasoning.

The question is whether or not this phenomenon is local or more widespread. So, offering the hypothesis that this pattern will be seen in other environments where these beetles are found, the scientist goes forth to collect specimens elsewhere. If, in other environments, the same pattern is seen, the scientist has support for the view that the pattern is related to the species not to the environment. If the pattern is not found in other environments, then the hypothesis is rejected and the conclusion is reached that the coloring on the males and females varies based on location.

It is important to note that since it would be impossible to survey all beetles in all locations, the acceptance of the hypothesis only gives support – not proof – to the original proposal. However, if beetles are found in some locations with color ratios that are different from those originally seen, it is possible to reject the proposed generalization. So, while it is not possible in science to prove that something is true, it is possible in science to demonstrate that something is false.

The classroom implications are clear. H/D reasoning is an important tool in science and students should be given opportunities to explore it. "The fact that science has at its core a general hypothetico-deductive research method suggests that a greater awareness of that method ... would improve the quality ... of science instruction" (Lawson, 2000, p. 492). Lawson also provides several useful examples of H/D reasoning for use in the science classroom including Harvey and blood flow, Loewi and nerve impulses, Lyells and the age of fossils, Young's work on the nature of light and atomic structure and Dalton. (WM)

Lawson, A. E. (2000). The generality of hypothetico-deductive reasoning: Making scientific thinking explicit. *American Biology Teacher, 62*(7), 482-495.

Oldroyd, D. R. (1986). *The arch of knowledge: An introductory study of the history of the philosophy and methodology of science.* New York, NY: Methuen.

Inclusive Science Education is science education that intends to reach *all* students, not just students who express an interest in or talent for science.

The desire to make science instruction more inclusive has come from various quarters including from advocates for special education students, those who have noticed the underrepresentation of women, minorities, those from a lower socio-economic background and others in science education and science careers. This issue has been addressed on a global scale by organizations such as UNESCO (United Nations Educational, Scientific, and Cultural Organization) who aim to educate students in science "despite socioeconomic level, race/ethnicity, cultural background, gender, religion, country of origin, sexual orientation, physical ability, intellectual ability, or home language" (UNESCO, 2012).

From the special education perspective in the United States, inclusive education, or inclusion, has come to be more narrowly defined as educating students with special educational needs, such as specific learning disabilities, alongside students without special needs so that they may have the right of participation in the science classroom. Advocates of inclusion have made efforts to promote instructional and cognitive strategies that result in positive student learning outcomes for children with learning and behavioral difficulties (Mastropieri & Scruggs, 2010).

Science teachers who aim to foster an inclusive classroom for students with special needs might engage in effective strategies such as collaboration with the special education teacher, peer tutoring, cooperative learning, integrating units, and concept mapping (Haskell, 2000).

Science teachers aiming for a more broad interpretation of inclusive science education work to help all of their students see themselves as scientists. These teachers use multiple strategies, including using examples of scientists that reflect the population of the students in the classroom, designing rigorous science lessons that are also relevant to students, modifying assignments, texts, and directions to make them accessible to students with language or learning needs, and creating a culture of discourse about science in the classroom. (AB)

Haskell, D. H. (2000). Building Bridges between Science and Special Education: Inclusion in the Science Classroom. *Electronic Journal of Science Education, 4*(3). Retrieved from http://ejse.southwestern.edu/article/view/7631

Mastropieri, M. A., & Scruggs, T. E. (2000). *The inclusive classroom*. New York, NY: Merrill.

UNESCO. (2012). *Inclusive education: Addressing exclusion*. Paris, France: Author. Retrieved from http://www.unesco.org/new/en/education/themes/strengthening-education-systems/inclusive-education

Induction (Inductive Thinking) is a type of reasoning (see also) used in science to create new laws and theories by which individual facts and observations are formed into general conclusions (patterns) or laws. Deduction (see also) is a complementary logical process used to tests ideas (McComas, 2004).

Inductive reasoning begins with patterns, regularities, and resemblances noted though experiences and observations that we assume exist independently of those observing them. These observations may be formed inductively into general principles that may have meaning beyond the instance. They may be simple, like the observation that sugar sweetens tea (leading to the conclusion that sugar sweetens all drinks) or complicated such as the movement of objects.

Oldroyd (1986) describes the relationship between induction and deduction as 'the arch of knowledge.' The arch begins with experiences or evidence to be explained. The arch generally rises through induction towards general statements that make sense of the evidence. "Along the arch the scientist applies the single basic standard of 'fit.' The explanatory theory must fit with all the relevant evidence so far" (Barnes, 2000, p. 184).

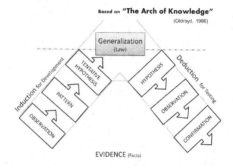

We use our past experiences when engaging in inductive reasoning. Inductive reasoning is so common that it regularly goes unnoticed (Tidman & Kahane, 2003). Induction can be problematic if we form conclusions without enough evidence and if we fail to continually evaluate current conclusions when new information becomes available. Conclusions formed from induction can never be proved (even with more evidence), but conclusions can be shown to be false. If a new species of an animal is found that is clearly a bird in all ways expect that it lacks feathers, we would have to reject our generalization that *all birds have feathers*. However, finding another new bird that has feathers does not "prove" the original generalization since a featherless bird might still exist somewhere.

Induction and deduction are central to the nature of science (see also), but the science education literature typically focuses on induction as a knowledge generating tool while deduction is rarely mentioned. Students should be given opportunities to use both as they explore the "arch of knowledge." (CB)

Barnes, H. M. (2000). *Stages of thought: The co-evolution of religious thought and science.* New York, NY: Oxford University Press.

McComas, W. F. (2004). Keys to teaching the nature of science: Focusing on the nature of science in the science classroom. *The Science Teacher, 71*(9), 24-27.

Oldroyd, D. R. (1986). *The arch of knowledge: An introductory study of the history of the philosophy an methodology of science.* New York, NY: Methuen.

Tidman, P. & Kahane, H. (2003). *Logic and philosophy* (9th ed.). Belmont, CA: Wadsworth/Thomson.

Inferences are possible hypotheses, conclusions or explanations based on data and/or observations.

We use the process of inference daily. If we see traffic slowing down ahead of us on the road, we may infer that there has been an accident because we know that there have been many accidents in the past that have slowed traffic. If we do not see evidence of the accident, our inference must be discarded. If we see wet footprints coming from a swimming pool we would logically infer that someone was recently using the pool. We must always remember that inferences are not evidence or even guaranteed to be accurate but are useful tools in making sense of data gained through observation (even though such observations are colored by the observer's prior experiences).

With this warning in mind, observations still may provide information collected through the use of senses and come in two types: quantitative (measurable or countable such as length, weight, and temperature) and qualitative (describable and not measurable such as color, smell, and taste). Inferences are conclusions or assumptions based on these observations or the process of making conclusions from a set of evidence (Jeffeys, 1931/1974).

When making inferences based on evidence, Townes et al (2001) tell us to be careful. They say "Any evidence ... is almost always 'incomplete, inconclusive, and amenable to multiple explanations.' ... Using evidence to make inferences—explanations, conclusions, or predictions based on what we know and observe—is always done in the presence of uncertainty" (p. 11).

Making inferences is only one aspect of effective reasoning (see also) and that making conclusions based on evidence also includes abduction (creative thinking), induction (see also), and deduction (see also) (Niiniluoto, 2004). Towns et al. (2001) says that inferential force "is created by moving among the data, explaining the warrants for each step in the inferential chain (see argumentation), and adding appropriate qualifiers and conditions" (p. 12).

Inferences are strengthened by making predictions and testing them, pursuing the best explanations by reviewing and rejecting alternative or competing hypotheses, describing unobserved explanations, and modifying predictions to account for unforeseen results or data.

In science classrooms it is important to give students opportunities to make inferences and to understand the difference between the inference and the data on which the inference was based. Students must also recognize that inferential thinking is just one kind of reasoning used in science and all conclusions gained from such thinking should be evaluated further when and if more evidence becomes available. (CB)

Jeffreys, H. (1974/1931). *Scientific inference*. Cambridge, UK: Cambridge University Press.
Niiniluoto, I. (2004). Truth-seeking abduction. In F. Stadler (Ed.), *Induction and deduction in the sciences* (pp. 57-82). Dordrecht, The Netherlands: Kluwer Academic Publishers.
Towne, L. Shavelson, R. J., & Feuer, M. J. (2001). *Science, evidence, and inference in education: Report of a workshop*. Washington, DC: National Academy Press.

Informal (Free Choice) Science Learning describes learning that occurs in environments outside of the school in contrast to the teacher-guided instruction within a school setting (McComas, 2006). Informal learning may occur with many sorts of self-selected activities; by visiting a museum, science center or zoo, the internet, by watching television and/or by reading.

Falk (2001) has suggested that the term "informal" should be replaced with "free choice learning," which is non-sequential, self-paced, and voluntary. It is guided by one's own needs and interests. In contrast to classroom experiences, "free choice learning experiences allow the learner the opportunity to stop at will, repeat at will, spend more or less time, and share the learning process with friends and family members" (p. 47).

No matter the label, there are differences between the way learners act and interact when they choose to learn on their own (typically out of school) and when someone else directs them in their learning (typically in school). The term informal learning became common in the 1970s when museum professionals and environmental educators wanted to distinguish between their activities and those in school-based settings. The distinction between formal and informal learning is now broadly accepted. People do not engage in informal learning to become science experts but to become more knowledgeable and motivated to learn in the future; this can lead to greater science literacy (Falk & Dierking, 2000).

It is difficult to measure what people learn in informal or free choice learning environments because of the open-ended nature of the learning in such settings. The visitor is free to learn whatever he/she wishes. Research indicates that learning in informal (free choice) environments may span all three domains; cognitive, affective, and psycho-motor domains (Meredith et al., 1997). Most classrooms focus on the cognitive or knowledge component while minimizing the emotional component (Falk & Dierking, 2000). Rennie and Johnston (2004) suggest that learning in informal settings is contextualized and takes time. No single visit to a science center or museum, for instance, can result in complete understanding of the featured phenomenon. In contrast to school, the learner does not have the advantage of a teacher as a guide and to check for understanding. (LW)

Falk, J. H. (2001). *Free choice science education: How we learn science outside of school.* New York: Teachers College Press.

Falk, J. H., & Dierking, L. D. (2000). *Learning from museums: Visitor experiences and the making of meaning.* Walnut Creek, CA: AltaMira Press.

McComas, W. F. (2006). Science teaching beyond the classroom: The role and nature of informal learning environments. *The Science Teacher, 73*(1), 26-30.

Meredith, J. E., Fortner, R. W., & Mullins, G. W. (1997). A model of affect in nonformal Education facilities. *Journal of Research in Science Teaching, 34*(8), 805-818.

Rennie, L. J., & Johnston, D. J. (2004). The nature of learning and its implications for research in learning from museums. *Science Education, 88 (Supplement),* S4-S16.

Inquiry Instruction is a general label for any instructional technique in which students are engaged in the investigation of scientifically oriented questions. Students seek evidence to address questions, develop explanations/answers to the questions posed, evaluate these explanations as well as potential alternative explanations, and communicate their conclusions (see Discovery Learning) (National Research Council [NRC], 2000). An additional consideration with respect to inquiry is that students must understand that scientists use inquiry in their work, thus science should be taught *as* inquiry as well as through inquiry.

Many experts in science education (NRC, 2000) suggest that inquiry should be included in science instruction at all grade levels and in every domain of science. Through inquiry learning, students learn science in a way that reflects how science actually works. Inquiry learning is a problem-solving technique with emphasis on the process of investigating the problem, rather than on reaching for a "correct" solution (Moore, 2009). Inquiry learning can be individual or collaborative. However, since scientists work in teams, it makes sense for students to work collaboratively. This encourages inquiry and discovery learning by incorporating co-construction of knowledge from the original learning situation but retains each partner's individual perspective to some degree (Wentzel & Watkins, 2011).

Table 1: A Continuum of Inquiry: Levels of Inquiry Instruction

	Level of Inquiry		
	Structured	Guided	Open (Authentic)
Who Picks the Problem?	Generated by teacher	Generated by teacher	Generated by students
Who Provides the Process for Solving the Problem?	Decided by teacher	Decided by students	Decided by students
Who Establishes the Answer or Solution to the Problem?	Determined by students	Determined by students	Determined by students

Structured, Guided and Open (Authentic) Inquiry: There are essentially three levels or kinds of inquiry learning each with its own strengths and limitations (see Table 1). The first, **structured inquiry** is the most teacher-orientated form. In structured inquiry the teacher provides the students with the problem and the method(s) to investigate it. The students follow the methods to investigate the teacher identified problem. The teacher can also identify the problem but allow the students to decide how to investigate it. This is referred to as **guided inquiry**. Finally, the teacher may use **open inquiry,** also referred to as **authentic inquiry**, in which the students are responsible for identifying the problem and designing ways to investigate it. Open inquiry is the least structured and most learner-centered level of inquiry. This open inquiry is the kind of research conducted by scientists (Bell et al.*, 2005; Colburn, 2000). The science fair (see also) represents the highest form of open inquiry.

In open-inquiry situations, the students identify problems (brainstorm and ask questions), work toward solutions (formulate questions, investigate, and analyze), and establish solutions (interpret results, discuss, reflect, make conclusions and present results) (Bruner, 2004).

Others have facilitated open inquiry using the four-question strategy by Cothran et al. (2000). For example, Wheeler and Bell (2012) demonstrated a method to help chemistry students answer their own research questions using the reaction of hydrochloric acid and aluminum foil. The activity was structured to accommodate the students' varied experience and comfort levels with the inquiry process. The researchers found that students were more engaged and took ownership of the activity as well as content. Teachers can scaffold inquiry into chemistry instruction with investigations already in use.

Context and student readiness are important considerations with respect to inquiry instruction. Some researchers argue that novice and intermediate learners should receive explicit guidance accompanied by practice and feedback (Clark et al., 2012) for effective learning to occur. They noted that students who learn science in classrooms with pure discovery or open inquiry methods and little feedback become lost and frustrated, and their confusion can lead to the development of misconceptions. These researchers argue that there is wisdom in using lots of guidance with novice learners and then fading that guidance as students gain mastery. Minimal guidance should be used to reinforce or practice previously learned material. On the surface it may seem the authors are criticizing inquiry, but they are actually supporting a continuum of structured inquiry to guided inquiry to open inquiry which is accompanied by feedback from teachers at the early stages of inquiry and by continuous student practice with inquiry skills.

Benefits of Inquiry: Inquiry based learning is associated with several positive features. One of the most powerful benefits of inquiry is that it can provide students a more accurate understanding of how science research is conducted, particularly if teachers draw students' attention to key aspects of the process in a way that makes students think about authentic science research. In addition, inquiry experiences may encourage students to develop creative solutions to problems, similar to the creativity found in authentic scientific pursuits. Inquiry learning affords students the chance to develop improved understanding of science concepts largely by providing a meaningful context for learning (Edelson et al., 1999). Because students are able to draw on varying skills throughout the flexible inquiry process, they can better recognize gaps in their content knowledge without fear of failure (Hiebert et al., 1996). When students recognize these gaps in their knowledge they often become more interested and curious and want to learn more about the problem. The inquiry process places a demand on the student to learn science content knowledge in order to successfully complete the investigation. By providing students the opportunity to pursue answers to their own questions, inquiry can lead them to find new scientific principles, refine prior knowledge, and even discover misconceptions as they investigate answers to the questions. Of course, there is always the chance that new misconceptions may be formed unless a teacher is attentive to this possibility. Finally, inquiry affords students the opportunity to apply their scientific understanding in the pursuit of research questions, allowing them to reinforce and enrich its connections to other knowledge.

Limitations of Inquiry: Despite the many benefits of inquiry learning, there are limitations that hinder its use in classroom settings. One essential challenge to inquiry teaching is that students may not have the science content background and pedagogical experiences necessary to support this teaching technique. Also, providing authentic inquiry instruction requires significant time commitment on the part of the teacher. Thinking of problems that have relevance to the students, providing resources for students to investigate the problems, and planning tools for assessment require extra time. Additionally, true inquiry-based instruction can seem chaotic. Some students finish quicker than other students which can be problematic for the teacher. Giving students the freedom to engage in problem solving is time consuming and is often at odds with the need to cover vast amounts of content for standardized testing requirements. (LW/WM)

Bell, R. L., Smetana, L., & Binns, I. (2005). Simplifying inquiry instruction. *The Science Teacher, 72*(7), 30-33.

Bruner, J. (2004). *Toward a theory of instruction.* Cambridge, MA: Belknap.

Clark, R., Kirschner, P., & Sweller, J. (2012). Putting students on the path to learning: The case for fully guided instruction. *American Educator, 36*(1), 6-11.

Colburn, A. (2000). An inquiry primer. *Science Scope, 23(6)*, 42-44.

Cothran, J. H., Geiss, R. N., & Rezba, R. J., (2000). *Students and research: Practical strategies for science classrooms and competitions.* Dubuque, Iowa: Kendall Hunt Publishing.

Edelson, D., Gordin, D. N., & Pea, R. D. (1999). Addressing the challenges of inquiry-based learning through technology and curriculum design. *The Journal of Learning Sciences, 8*(3/4), 391-450.

Hiebert, J., Carpenter, T. P., Fennema, E., Fuson, K., Human, P., et al. (1996). Problem solving as a basis for reform in curriculum and instruction: The case for mathematics. *Educational Researcher, 25*(4), 12-21.

Moore, K. (2009). *Effective instructional strategies.* Thousand Oaks, CA: Sage Publications.

National Research Council. (2000). *Inquiry and the National Science Education Standards.* Washington, DC: National Academy Press.

Wentzel, K. R., & Watkins, D. E. (2011). Chapter 16: Instruction based on peer interactions. In R. E. Mayer & P. A. Alexander (Eds.), *Handbook of research on learning and instruction.* New York, NY: Routledge.

Wheeler, L., & Bell, R. (2012). Open-ended inquiry: Practical ways of implementing inquiry in the chemistry classroom. *The Science Teacher, 79*(6), 32-39.

Laboratory and Science Teaching is either a place where student investigations are conducted or the investigations and activities themselves. Laboratory work in school science is also called "practical work" by some and includes "dry" labs, "wet" labs and levels of student choice in making decisions about how to conduct laboratory investigations

Hegarty-Hazel (1990, p. 4) defines the laboratory as any environment "where students engage in planned learning experiences, and interact with materials to observe and understand phenomena." Anderson (1976, p. 7) adds that the school science laboratory is a place "where students can investigate natural phenomena in an immediate or first-hand experience and apply various cognitive skills toward an interpretation of these phenomena." These definitions consider the laboratory a learning place but one that is not limited to a specific room in the school called the "laboratory." (See outdoor education, informal science, and situated learning).

The term "laboratory" has several meanings. For instance, a laboratory could be a specific room in a school (such as the physics laboratory) or the "laboratory" could be a museum, park, nature center or even the school yard. Students should be encouraged to see and experience science in these diverse settings either facilitated by teachers or when working on their own. Also, when students learn something new by investigating, playing with objects and processes, or observing and interacting in the natural world, they could also be said to have learned in a laboratory setting. Finally, the term "laboratory" could be used to refer to a particular activity. For instance, if students are experimenting with acids and bases in science class they could be said to be doing a "chemistry laboratory."

Laboratory Level and Student Decision Making   One element of the laboratory that has been shown to impact students is the degree to which students make decisions and choices about how to do the work. Generally, as students are given more choices, their attitudes and learning improves (Leonard, 1980). Table 1 illustrates some of the ways that decision making in the laboratory activity can be open for student choice.

Table 1: Schwab (1962) Herron (1971) Levels of Student Choice in the Laboratory based on whether the teacher or the students makes decisions about particular elements of the investigation.

Level	Question(s)	Procedure	Answers
0	Given	Given	Given
1	Given	Given	Open
2	Given	Open	Open
3	Open	Open	Open

In Level 0 and 1 labs, the work is considered "cookbook." In both cases, students just follow instructions, the difference being that in level 0 the students already know the answer because they are just confirming something already available in the textbooks. With a Level 3 activity, the students act like real scientists by

55

selecting a question, designing a procedure and collecting data and then thinking about the answer to the question.

Included below are a number of additional definitions associated with the practice of science teaching in the laboratory. Note that these are not mutually exclusive terms. For instance, one could have students perform a "dry / cookbook lab."

"Dry" Laboratory activities are those that do not use real laboratory equipment but simulate aspects of the actual observation or experiment either using technology or with paper and pencil or cut-out materials. A popular "dry lab" in biology class is one in which students build a model of DNA cut from a diagram printed on paper. The students can then simulate how one strand of DNA can bond with the other strand by moving pieces of paper into place so that "A" bonds with "T" and "C" bonds with "G." In another example, students receive a map of the earth showing the plate boundaries and are asked to cut the map along these boundaries. Moving these map pieces can demonstrate various geologic phenomena and explain why earthquakes and volcanoes occur where they do. Although some teachers reject the use of "dry labs," they do have a place in science teaching to illustrate important concepts; however they do not help build real-world laboratory skills.

"Wet" Laboratory investigations are the more traditional laboratory exercises that do permit students to use real laboratory equipment to investigate phenomena and explore nature. There are countless examples of such labs including the use of the microscopes in biology class, an exploration of chemical bonding by doing experiments with actual compounds and elements in chemistry class, and a variety of explorations of speed and velocity with actual cars, ramps and timers in physics. The advantage in using "wet labs" is that students gain expertise in using actual laboratory equipment and experience some of the frustrations scientists encounter when working with real world data. Of course, with real data comes real complexity and this often requires teachers to interact with students to assist them in sense-making.

Virtual Science Laboratories, which may also be called a "collaboratory" is a "center without walls, in which the nation's researchers can perform their research without regard to geographical location" (Wulf, 1993, p. 854). These laboratories strive to maintain an open environment where scientists from various disciplines can use and share leading-edge technology and can collaborate via the virtual world through a worldwide collection of networked computers. Virtual laboratories provide not only the opportunity for scientists to communicate and share data but also to share high-tech or remote instrumentation such as a large telescope or an instrument surveying the ocean floor. As with physical laboratories, virtual science labs "are social spaces in which scientists interact, organize into groups, develop relationships, and share opinions, ideas, resources, and work" (Chin et al., 2002, p. 92). In a high school physics classroom, students might work in a virtual lab with students from another school to complete investigations covering 'freely falling objects' or' 'energy conservation.' Within the virtual framework, students from these different regions can share the virtual tools, discuss core concepts, analyze data, and reflect on the results together (Yang & Heh, 2007).

"Cookbook" Laboratory activities give students a step-by-step set of instructions for doing the work, much like following a recipe in a cookbook in preparing a meal. These activities are typically Level 0 or 1 in terms of student choice. The "cookbook" laboratory activity has been widely criticized yet still remains in wide use in teaching school science.

McComas (2005) offers a number of suggestions to improve laboratory teaching (also called practical work). The use of long term activities rather than simple single class experiences can show students how science works in the real world. This is also true if science investigations were to take place outside the school thus demonstrating that investigations may occur in a variety of places. Educators should use laboratory activities to introduce topics rather than having the laboratory simply demonstrate something already discussed in class. Teachers might also give students opportunities to make personal decisions rather than follow a set of step-by-step instructions thus raising the "level" of the laboratory.

Finally, it is important that teachers not refer to every activity done in science class as a "laboratory." It is preferable to use this label only for experiments, observations and inquiry experiences (see also). There is value in having students engage in all kinds of hands-on work (see also) but if the activity requires no true exploration and no opportunity for students to make predictions and provide conclusions; it would be best to call these activities rather than laboratories. An extensive examination of the role of the laboratory in school science is found in *America's Lab report: Investigations in School Science* (Singer et al., 2005). (WM)

Anderson, O. R. (1976). The experience of science. *Mathematics Teacher, 93*(6), 504-510.
Chin, G., Myers, J., & Hoyt, D. (2002). Social networks in the virtual science laboratory. *Communications of the ACM, 45*(8), 87-92.
Hegarty-Hazel, E. H. (1990). Tertiary science classrooms. In E. H. Hegarty-Hazel (Ed.), *The student laboratory and the science curriculum* (pp. 357-382). New York: Routledge.
Herron, M. D. (1971). The nature of scientific inquiry. *School Review (American Journal of Education), 68*(1), 17-29.
Leonard, W. H. (1980). Using an extended discretion approach in biology laboratory investigations.*The American Biology Teacher, 42*(7), 338-348.
McComas, W. F. (2005). Laboratory instruction in the service of science teaching and learning. *The Science Teacher, 72*(7), 24-29.
Schwab, J. J. (1962). The teaching of science as inquiry. In J. J. Schwab & P. F. Brandwein, *The teaching of science* (pp. 3-103). Cambridge, MA: Harvard University Press.
Singer, S. R., Hilton, M. L., & Schwiengruber, H. A. (Eds.). (2005). *America's lab report: Investigations in school science.* Washington, DC: National Academies Press.
Wulf, W. (1993). The collaboratory opportunity. *Science, 261*(5121), 854-855.
Yang, K., & Heh, K. (2007). The impact of internet virtual physics laboratory instruction on the achievement in physics, science process skills, and computer attitudes of 10th-grade students. *Journal of Education Technology, 16*(5), 451-461.

Law (Scientific Law or Principle) is "a descriptive generalization [i.e. a pattern] about how some aspect of the natural world behaves under stated circumstances" (National Academy of Sciences, 1998, p. 5).

A scientific law is a basic principle, generalization, regularity or rule that holds true universally under particular conditions. Laws are developed from facts or developed mathematically to explain and predict individual occurrences or instances (Carey, 1994; Carnap, 1966; Mayer, 1988). For example, the law of gravity predicts the force of attraction between two objects given the masses of the objects and the distances between them, but does not explain why that law functions as it does. Theories (see also) explain why laws function as they do.

The definition of "law" includes the following aspects (McComas, 2003).

- are tested using hypothetico-deductive logic (this means that predictions are made based on the law and if such predictions occur, the law is considered to be accurate);
- are supported by and based on many facts, experiments, and observations;
- relate cause and effect relationships (some would say, universally);
- explain why particular *instances* occur (ex. objects fall at a particular speed *because* of the law of gravity);
- predict future instances or occurrences of the relationship;
- are considered to be discovered using induction rather than invented

There are countless laws found throughout the sciences such as *Boyle's Law* in physics, the *Periodic Law* in chemistry and *Mendel's Laws* in biology. One distinction regarding laws in these areas relates to how universal they may be. In other words, do these laws operate in exactly the same fashion everywhere? In biology, many laws operate less well and offer less secure predictions than in other sciences. For example, a law called *Bergman's Body Rule* states that animals in colder regions are fatter than related animals in warmer regions. This is a useful law but it functions only about 75% of the time. Laws in chemistry and physics generally operate closer to 100%.

Unfortunately, teachers and textbooks often say that laws are more important than theories, even stating that theories will become laws when more experiments and facts support them. Both statements are untrue; laws and theories are equally important tools and products of science but one does not become the other. (WM)

Carey, S. S. (1994). *A beginner's guide to scientific method*. Belmont, CA: Wadsworth Publishing Co.

Carnap, R. (1966). *Philosophical foundations of physics*. New York: Basic Books.

Mayer, E. (1988). *Toward a new philosophy of biology*. Cambridge, MA: Belknap Press.

McComas, W. F. (2003). A textbook case: Laws and theories in biology instruction. *International Journal of Science and Mathematics Education, 1*(2), 1-15.

McComas, W. F. (2004). Keys to teaching the nature of science: Focusing on the nature of science in the science classroom. *The Science Teacher, 71*(9), 24-27.

National Academy of Sciences. (1998). *Teaching about evolution and the nature of science*. Washington, DC: National Academy Press.

Learning Cycle relates to one of several instructional models based on notions about how people learn. Several learning cycles have been proposed for science instruction. The most important historic model is the three step version of Atkin and Karplus (1962) while the 5E model (Bybee, 2006) is the most commonly used recent model.

The earliest learning cycle instructional model for science known as guided discovery was proposed by Karplus and Atkin (1962) and was based on the work of Jean Piaget. In this three step model, students are encouraged to form their own new reasoning patterns of a scientific concept from their interaction with phenomena and ideas of others. This model was based on the important consideration that concrete experiences are vital for learning and should be used before and during the learners' concept development. This pedagogical model facilitates learners to extend scientific knowledge by applying it in daily life and allowing their scientific knowledge to last (Nuhoğlu & Yalçin, 2006).

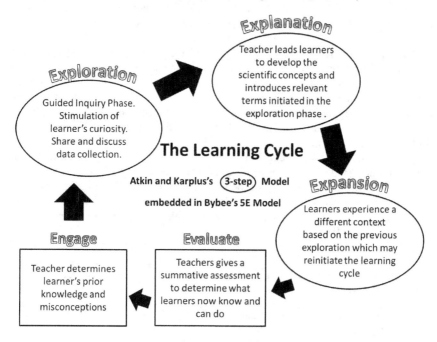

The three-step learning cycle phases are: *exploration* (concept exploration), *explanation* (concept development), and *expansion* (concept application). *Exploration* phase, the crucial part of the theoretical bases of the learning cycle, is the phase when learners' curiosity is stimulated. In this phase, cognitive dissonance occurs, and learners share and discuss their data collection. *Explanation* is the phase when the teacher assists students in developing and understanding the targeted science ideas and then labels them once understanding has been achieved. *Expansion* is the phase when learners face a new problem or situation identified in their *exploration* phase, and they can apply the concept that they learned from the *explanation* phase to solve it. In this phase, the teacher facilitates the use of the concepts in different contexts which may initiate the learning cycle again for the learner (Abraham & Renner, 1986).

In a biology classroom, for example, a teacher may plan a lesson to measure the metabolic rate of *Daphnia,* tiny freshwater animals. During the *exploration* phase, students might count the number of heart beats per minute at various temperatures and graph their findings. They might also observe or identify a pattern of regularity such as an increasing heart rate with increasing temperature. During the second phase, the teacher, a textbook, a video, or some other medium might introduce new terms such as cold-blooded metabolism or the formal term of "poikilotherm." In the final stage, expansion, students could be asked to determine the metabolic type of a different species (Lawson, 2001).

Recently, Roger Bybee (2006) reflecting on the importance of students' prior ideas in learning has built on the traditional three step model and established the 5-step or 5E model: engage, explore, explain, elaborate, and evaluate. In the first step, *engage*, the teacher tries to determine what the students already know or think they know about the concepts and topics to be covered in the lesson or unit. The second step, *explore*, of the 5E model is the same as the first step in the 3-phase model, *exploration*. Students interact with ideas and materials by asking questions, observing, describing, recording, comparing and sharing their ideas, experiences, and data. The 3rd step, *explain*; in the 5E model is the same as the 2nd phase in the 3-phase mode, *explanation*. Students are introduced to scientific terms, formal language, and content knowledge about the current topic. During the next step of the 5E model, students are performing the same objectives as in the *expansion* phase of the 3-phase model by deepening their understanding of processes and concepts from application into new situations or problems. The last 5E step, *evaluate*, provides a summative assessment (see also) of what students now know and can do. (SI/CB)

Abraham, M. R., & Renner, J. W. (1986). The sequence of learning cycle activities in high school chemistry. *Journal of Research in Science Teaching, 23*(2), 121-143.

Atkin, J. M., & Karplus, R. (1962). Discovery or invention? The *Science Teacher, 29*(5), 45-51.

Bybee, R. W. (2006). How inquiry could contribute to the prepared mind. *The American Biology Teacher, 68*(8), 454-457.

Lawson, A. E. (2001). Using the learning cycle to teach biology concepts and reasoning patterns. *Journal of Biological Education, 35*(4), 165-170.

Nuhoğlu, H., & Yalçin, N. (2006). The effectiveness of the learning cycle model to increase students' achievement in the physics laboratory. *Journal of Turkish Science Education, 3*(2), 28-30.

Learning Progression is a teaching plan based on the notion that students must explore and learn some ideas before others in order to fully understand a scientific concept or practice. Many research initiatives are presently focused on determining the necessary intermediate stages leading to comprehensive knowledge in science.

Students can gain clearer understanding of a concept or practice in the science classroom by moving from simpler to more complex examples or models (Schwarz et al., 2009). Therefore, a learning progression typically begins as teachers discuss what students already know (see constructivism). This is important so that students can build understanding as they integrate new content with prior knowledge and experiences (Krajcik et al., 2008). The first step encourages the student to find the meaning behind the concept or practice in order to establish a firm connection to the learning opportunity. Asking students to explore the origin or history of the topic is a great place to begin this connection. Giving examples and relevant current events that relate to the topic can provide illustrations for students to expand on the connection. Many science educators suggest that students should engage in scientific practices (Duschl et al., 2007).

A useful way to encourage this participation is the use of the learning progression. For example, when introducing a practice such as scientific modeling (see also) it is best to begin with a simple illustration. Teachers might have students draw concept maps (see also) related to plant growth. This would help to show what students already know about the topic. The first model would likely include what is visible to students such as water and sunlight. The next step in the progression is to examine trends of plant growth that happen in response to differing levels of these elements. Students can then see how the intensity and frequency of each element plays a role in plant growth. From this experience, students comprehend that the mere presence of sunlight and water is not the only determining factor to plant growth. Following this exercise, more complex instruction would include a discussion of nutrients, climate conditions, and genetics that also determine plant development.

Learning progressions can span multiple years of education as science educators provide the learning opportunities that allow for opening the student mindset to a complete understanding. (JK)

Duschl, R. A., Schweingruber, H. A., & Shouse, A. W. (Eds.). (2007). *Taking science to school: Learning and teaching science in grades K-8.* Washington, DC: National Academies Process.

Krajcik, J., McNeill, K. L., & Reiser, B. J. (2008). Learning-goals-driven design model, Developing curriculum materials that align with national standards and incorporate project-based pedagogy. *Science Education, 92*(1), 1-32.

Schwarz, C. V., Reiser, B. J., Davis, E. A., Kenyon, L., Archer, A., Fortus, D., Shwartz, Y., Hug, B., & Krajcik, J. (2009). Developing a learning progression for scientific modeling: Making scientificmodeling accessible and meaningful for learners. *Journal of Research in Science Teaching, 46*(6), 632-654.

Meaning Making and Science Learning relates to the thinking processes that students use to make sense of the world around them particularly with respect to some specific phenomenon or event. Meaning making occurs both in and out of school but the term is most frequently used to describe learning in informal (non-school) science learning environments (see also) (Falk & Dierking, 2000).

"Meaning making" may be thought of as the "sense making" that occurs when an individual interacts with new information, objects, ideas, experiences and/or images and incorporates them into his or her prior understanding in a mechanism that most would call constructivist (see also).

"Meaning making" is related to the process of "making sense of the world" but it does not tell us much about *how* that sense-making occurs within the learner or observer. So, meaning making is a description of what is happening within learners as they encounter new ideas and experiences, but various experts have their own ideas about how this process takes place. One group, Cranton and King (2003), for instance, may use the term "meaning making" to refer to *Mezirow's Theory of Transformative Learning* which includes an examination of the way a person thinks about the self, their beliefs and their lifestyle. Others may link "meaning making" with learning theorists such as Dewey, Piaget and/or Vygotsky (Scott, 1998). Still others, Falk and Dierking (2000) and Silverman (2010) drew on various models, including constructivism, in their explanation of how people make sense of what they see and experience.

The term "meaning making" is a general term that refers to the process of evaluating, considering, and incorporating any new experience by an individual and could easily pertain to learning in any discipline. Considering "meaning making" in science learning may be most important since individuals typically have prior knowledge gained through their own experiences with the natural world. Of course, meaning-making occurs in schools settings, but consider this example from the informal world. When a young child enters a science museum, for instance, they will have some ideas about nature. As a student walks through the re-creation of a tropical jungle they will "make meaning" of that ecosystem in personal ways. A student who may have had no personal experience with the tropics will see and experience the simulated museum environment very differently than students from Indonesia who may have actually been to such environment or even live there. Both students will gain some understanding – but different understanding – having spent time in the tropical environment created in a museum. (WM)

Cranton, P., & King, K. P. (2003). Transformative learning as a professional development goal. *New Directions for Adult and Continuing Education, 98*(1), 31-37.

Falk, J. H., & Dierking, L. D. (2000). *Learning from museums: Visitor experiences and the making of meaning.* Lanham: MD Altamira Press.

Scott, P. (1998). Teacher talk and meaning making in science classrooms: A Vygotskian analysis and review. *Studies in Science Education, 32*(1), 45-80.

Silverman, L. H. (2010). Visitor meaning-making in museums for a new age. *Curator, 38*(3), 161-170.

Metacognition is the process of thinking about one's own thinking, or the act of monitoring and controlling one's thoughts and cognitive processes while learning and knowing what strategies are personally useful to carry out any task more effectively.

Individuals who employ metacognition plan their learning or problem solving, evaluate their progress, and change tactics when necessary, often automatically (Martinez, 2006). Psychologists Flavell and Brown popularized the term *metacognition* through their writing and research in the late 1970s but were not the first to discuss processes that would eventually be labeled as metacognitive. In their theories of how students think, Vygotsky and Piaget separately outlined metacognitive processes or strategies that children learn from peers or adults, such as self-regulation by watching and listening to others and challenging the thoughts or ideas of peers.

Flavell refers to metacognition as "one's knowledge concerning one's own cognitive processes or anything related to them, e.g., the learning-relevant properties of information or data" (1976, p 232). Cognitive psychologist John Bransford and his colleagues (2000) define metacognition as "people's abilities to predict their performances on various tasks ... and to monitor their current levels of mastery and understanding" (p. 12). In fact, metacognition is included as one of their three key findings about learning: "A metacognitive approach to instruction can help students learn to take control of their own learning by defining learning goals and monitoring their progress in achieving them" (p. 18). Not only does this approach with students result in more self-regulated learners with a wider range of metacognitive skills, but Bransford and colleagues argue that it also strengthens students' ability to transfer the knowledge gained to other situations (p. 12).

The implications of these findings for the science classroom is that educators should teach children to use metacognitive strategies and do so in a way that is part of the content's curriculum, not taught separately (White and Frederickson, 1998) since the type of cognitive strategy may vary by subject area. Science teachers can guide students through metacognitive strategies such as sense-making, reflection, and self-assessment processes while employing explicit instruction, modeling and guided practice, and gradual release of responsibility, as well as peer discussion and collaboration to bolster metacognition. (AB)

Bransford, J., National Research Council (U.S.)., & National Research Council (U.S.). (2000). *How people learn: Brain, mind, experience, and school*. Washington, DC: National Academy Press.

Flavell, J. H. (1976). Metacognitive aspects of problem-solving. In L. B. Resnick (Ed.), *Perspectives on the development of memory and cognition* (pp. 231-235). Hillsdale, NJ: Lawrence Erlbaum Associates.

Martinez, M. E. (May 1, 2006). What is metacognition? *Phi Delta Kappan, 87*(9), 696-699.

White, B.Y., & Frederickson, J. R. (1998). Inquiry, modeling, and metacognition: Making science accessible to all students. *Cognition and Science, 16*(63), 90-91.

Micro-computer Based Laboratory (MBL) along with Computer-Based Laboratory (CBL) and Calculator-Based Ranger (CBR) refer to the use of devices (connected to computers or with built-in computer technology) that use various data collection devices (called probes; see also) to gather, store, and process information usually from a laboratory (see also) investigation in the science classroom. These devices (MBL, CBL and CBR) may assist in laboratory work by immediately displaying charts and graphs of collected information.

Modern curriculum frameworks (see also) and standards (see also) emphasize that students should actively communicate efficiently, solve complex problems, analyze information, and design solutions. Although teachers can integrate these types of skills into classrooms and into science laboratories without computer-based technologies, "nearly two decades of research has shown that students can make significant gains when computers are incorporated into labs" (Roschelle et al., 2000, p. 78) using MBLs because these types of laboratory modules can easily analyze data and display data in various formats.

One major advantage and a major challenge associated with MBLs is the ability of these devices to create and display graphical representations of data collected in real time (Brasell, 1987). Roschelle et al. (2000) point out that "Students no longer have to go home to laboriously plot points on a graph and then bring the graphs back to school the following day" (p. 79). Brasell (1987) discovered that even a 20 second delay between the graphical display and the conclusion of the measured event has an impact on learners' ability to link the concept with the graph. However there is concern that by automating data display students may not have enough time to process and incorporate what they have learned.

In addition to the ease and speed of display, a second advantage is that students investigating science concepts using MLBs can collect data in the environment. For example, in biology, students can take a field trip to a nearby creek or other natural water source, and through the use of MBLs, students can collect and measure pH, oxygenation, and other measures of the health of the water supply. Without the pHMLB devices, students would return to the classrooms with test tubes full of water samples, spend days dripping indicator solutions into the water samples, and then have to chart and hand graph the outcomes (Roschelle et al., 2000). (CB)

Brasell, H. (1987). The effects of real-time laboratory graphing on learning graphic representations of distance and velocity. *Journal of Research in Science Teaching, 24*(4), 385-395.

Roschelle, J. M., Pea, R. D., Hoadley, C. M., Gordin, D. N., & Means, B. M. (2000). Changing how and what children learn in school with computer-based technologies. *Children and Computer Technology, 10*(2), 76-101.

Misconceptions are ideas that students have that are different from those generally accepted by scientists (Odom & Barrow, 1995). Most refer to faulty ideas as misconceptions while the term "alternative conception or alternative idea" might be used as a label when the student holds a differing perspective that might be context dependent. Such views, whether misconception or alternative view are important in science teaching because such ideas might block or confuse future learning.

Science misconceptions are formed easily and can be very challenging to teachers. A common student misconception is that rocks are very heavy. When a teacher presents a student with a rock such as pumice, which is very light, the student may have a difficult time accepting this as a rock because it does not fit into their original concept. They have created an alternative conception of the properties of rocks based on their interactions in the environment and perhaps from prior teaching. Most likely a teacher has never directly told the student all rocks are heavy but the examples students have been exposed to have this property and they formed this view. Even the way we use language can cause misconceptions. We frequently talk about the Sun rising in the east, yet in reality, the sun does not rise or set at all; it is the earth's daily rotation that causes the sun to appear in the eastern sky each morning.

It is very important for a science teacher to understand what misconceptions a student may possess so the teacher can know how to direct instruction. There are a variety of web resources available to teachers to identify general misconceptions that students may have regarding science subjects along with a database developed in conjunction with Project 2061 containing assessment items teachers can use to determine common misconceptions among students (Larkin, 2012). Perhaps the easiest way to determine what students already know *before* beginning instruction is simply to talk with students, engage the students in some sort of advance organizer (see also) activity or administer a short quiz or questionnaire that would reveal students' prior knowledge. Once teachers identify key misconceptions, they can work to rebuild the knowledge so that the student's alternative concept is replaced with the correct information. (KM)

Larkin, D. (2012). Misconceptions about 'misconceptions': Preservice secondary science teachers' views on the value and role of student ideas. *Science Education, 96*(5), 927-959.
Odom, A. L., & Barrow, L. H. (1995). Development and application of a two-tier diagnostic test measuring college biology students' understanding of diffusion and osmosis after a course of instruction. *Journal of Research in Science Teaching, 32*(1), 45-61.

The *National Science Education Standards* (NSES) developed by the National Research Council in the United States is one of two major science curriculum documents (see also *Benchmarks for Science Literacy*) published in the mid-1990s to guide K-12 science curriculum development and classroom teaching.

The National Research Council desired a system of science standards available for all of those involved in science instruction from students in elementary school and high schools, to policy makers, administrators, and science teachers (Bybee, 1995). One interesting element of the NCES document is that the science content goals are accompanied by a strong focus on inquiry-based learning (see also) and considerations for teaching and assessment along with program standards for schools and districts. The standards were not intended to be "a how-to book" (Collins, 1998).

A national group of scientists and educators developed the NSES, but these standards were not endorsed by or created for the federal United States Department of Education. In the U.S., the individual states have control over most education matters. Thus, unlike most countries, the United States does not have mandatory national standards to guide science instruction. This remains true today even with the recently released Next Generation Science Standards (see also) designed to replace the NSES.

The NSES science content presents examples for procedural and conceptual scientific literacy. These examples indicate fundamental concepts, amount and type of vocabulary, and skills that all students should cultivate. The NSES suggest that science education must reach all students and that all students – regardless of background, intellectual ability, or interest in science – can and should learn science. NSES has also sparked discussions about what constitutes effective teaching, what science content and skills are of most importance, and that science should be taught using inquiry-based instruction (Rodriguez, 1996). (CB)

Bybee, R. W. (1995). Achieving scientific literacy. *The Science Teacher, 62*(7), 28.
Collins, A. (1998). National science education standards. A political document. *Journal of Research in Science Teaching, 35*(7), 711-727.
National Research Council. (1996). *National Science Education Standards*. Washington, DC: The National Academies Press.
Rodriguez, A. J. (1996). The dangerous discourse of invisibility: A critique of the National Research Council's National Science Education Standards. *Journal of Research in Science Teaching, 34*(1), 19-37.

Nature of Science (NOS) is that element of the science curriculum in which students learn how science functions, how scientific knowledge is generated and tested, and how scientists do their work (McComas et al., 1998).

There is no debate regarding the importance of including NOS in the science curriculum, but some suggest that it would be best to call this domain *Nature of Science Studies, History and Philosophy of Science (HPS), Ideas-about-Science, Nature of Sciences, Nature of Scientific Knowledge,* or *Views on the Nature of Science.* However, Nature of Science (NOS) is the most common label for this aspect of science instruction.

There are many rationales for the inclusion of NOS in science instruction but the list offered by Driver et al. (1996) remains a complete set of such rationales. They state that NOS in the science curriculum as a *utilitarian* function (permits students to make sense of science), a *democratic* element (fosters informed decision making regarding scientific issues, add to *cultural understanding* (since science is part of contemporary culture); has a *moral dimension* (provides understanding of how the scientific community functions) and adds to *science learning* (by enhancing the understanding of science content).

Much has been written about how best to teach the nature of science and a review of this literature would be prohibitively lengthy. However, Lederman and Niess (1997), Khishefe et al. (2002); Abd-El-Khalick (2001) have shown that effective NOS instruction must be explicit and involve students reflection. This means that NOS is communicated directly and clearly, usually within the context of the science subject, rather than assumed to be transferred indirectly as students are learning science content. NOS must be a clear learning goal given prominence in the classroom along with traditional science content.

A number of suggestions have been made regarding what NOS should be the focus in science classrooms. Osbourn and colleagues (2003), and Lederman (2002) have offered recommendations similar to those provided by McComas (2004, 2008), listed here within three main categories. This is not a list to be memorized by students but is designed as a guide to teachers as a set of NOS elements that students should have opportunities to learn, experience, test and even debate.

Science Shares Common Tools and Products
1) Science produces, demands, and relies on empirical evidence.
2) Knowledge production in science shares many common factors: shared habits of mind, norms, logical thinking, and methods such as careful observation and data recording, truthfulness in reporting, etc.
3) Laws and theories are related but are different types of scientific knowledge.

Science has Important Human Elements
4) Science has a creative component.
5) Scientific observations, ideas, and conclusions are not entirely objective and are directed, in part, by ones prior conceptions.
6) Historical, cultural, and social influences impact the practice and direction of science.

Scientific Knowledge has Limits
7) Science, technology and engineering impact each other but are not the same.
8) Scientific knowledge is tentative, durable, yet is self-correcting. (This means that science cannot prove anything except that scientific conclusions are valuable and long lasting because of the way in which they are developed; errors will be discovered and corrected as a standardize part of the scientific process).
9) Science and its methods cannot answer all questions. In other words, there are limits on the kinds of questions that can and should be asked within a scientific framework.

These particular NOS learning goals are recommended for inclusion in the science curriculum for several reasons. They are frequently mentioned by science education experts, function across all science disciplines, do not represent an undue burden on the science curriculum and are generally understandable by teachers and students. The *Next Generation Science Standards* (see also) released in the spring of 2013 in the United States have improved on past such documents. In the NGSS, NOS is featured in dedicated appendix on this topic and refer to NOS in association with the grade level science learning goals. (WM)

Abd-El-Khalick, F. (2001). Embedding nature of science instruction in preservice elementary science courses: Abandoning scientism, but... *Journal of Science Teacher Education, 12*(3), 215-233.

Driver, R., Leach, J., Millar, R., & Scott, P. (1996). *Young people's images of science.* Buckingham, UK: Open University Press.

Khishfe, R., & Abd-El-Khalick, F. (2002). Influence of explicit and reflective versus implicit inquiry-oriented instruction on sixth graders' views of nature of science. *Journal of Research in Science Teaching, 39*(7), 551-578.

Lederman, N.G. (2002). The state of science education: Subject matter without context. *Electronic Journal of Science Education* [On-Line], *3*(2). http://unr.edu/homepage/jcannon/ejse/ejse.html

Lederman, N.G ., & Niess, M. L. (1997). The nature of science: Naturally? *School Science and Mathematics, 97*(1), 1-2.

McComas, W. F. (2004). Keys to teaching the nature of science: Focusing on the nature of science in the science classroom. *The Science Teacher, 71*(9), 24-27.

McComas, W. F. (2008). Proposals for core nature of science content in popular books on the history and philosophy of science: Lessons for science education. In Y. J. Lee & A. L. Tan (Eds.), *Science education at the nexus of theory and practice*. Rotterdam: Sense Publishers.

McComas, W. F., Clough, M. P., & Almazroa, H. (1998). A review of the role and character of the nature of science in science education. In W. F. McComas (Ed.), *Nature of science in science education: Rationales and strategies* (pp. 3-39). Dordrecht: Kluwer (Springer) Academic Publishers.

Osborne, J., Collins, S., Ratcliffe, M., Millar, R., & Duschl, R. (2003). What "ideas-about-science" should be taught in school science? A Delphi Study of the Expert Community. *Journal of Research in Science Teaching, 40*, 692-720. DOI:10.1002/tea.10105.

Next Generation Science Standards **(NGSS)**, released in 2013, are a set of performance expectations designed to be adopted for use by K-12 science learners across the United States. In the U.S. each state makes individual decisions about which standards to use so there are no "national" educational standards. However, many states have shown interest in adopting the NGSS as the first set of widely shared educational goals with respect to science instruction (Achieve, 2013).

These standards were inspired by *A Framework for K-12 Science Education*, which was developed by the National Research Council (NRC) and released in July 2011. The Framework outlined the science and engineering practices, disciplinary core practices, and the crosscutting concepts necessary for all students to know and be able to do before their K-12 science education is complete. The organizations who led the development of the science standards – the National Research Council, the National Science Teachers Association, the American Association for the Advancement of Science, and Achieve (a nonprofit education reform organization) – developed the Standards through several rounds of drafts prepared by writing teams representing the states. Key stakeholders and the science education community have extensively reviewed the standards.

Although there are existing standards such as the *National Science Education Standards* from the U.S. National Research Council (NRC) and *Benchmarks for Science Literary* from the American Association for the Advancement of Science (AAAS) that have guided the states in their development of standards and assessments, these documents are over 15 years old and much has changed in the field of science in that time. Also, these documents were used as starting places for each state's standards whereas *the Next Generation Science Standards* can and should be used as-is for each state that chooses to implement the standards, leading to greater alignment across the nation. However, as the U.S. federal government has not been involved in the funding, development, implementation, or accountability for the use of the standards, it is unclear how extensively the standards will be used nationwide.

If a state decides to use the standards, the high-quality implementation of the NGSS relies on classroom teachers' use of the standards to plan units, lessons, and assessments. To make the NGSS document and online resources easily navigable by teachers, the standards are arranged and searchable by topic (chemical reactions, forces and interactions, weather and climate, etc.) and disciplinary core ideas (earth and space science, life science, etc.). However, the NGSS does not specify a curriculum for teachers, so states and districts across the United States will be responsible for providing detailed guidance for implementation to teachers. (AB)

Achieve, Inc. (2013). *The Next Generation Science Standards*. Washington, DC: Author. Retrieved from http://www.nextgenscience.org/next-generation-science-standards.

National Research Council (U.S.). (2011). *A framework for K-12 science education: Practices, crosscutting concepts, and core ideas*. Washington, DC: National Academies Press.

Outdoor Science Education refers to learning activities that occur outside of traditional classrooms in camps, on the school grounds, or within the community (Broda, 2007). Outdoor education can also mean education in, about, and the study of the "out-of-doors" (Ford, 1986; Priest, 1986) and is one example of a situated learning experience (see also) and informal science learning (see also).

Before classrooms, textbooks, and professional educators, students acquired knowledge from direct personal experiences (Hammerman, 1978) including those in the out of doors. According to Broda (2007), outdoor education is a type of experiential learning (see also) that uses authentic (real-world) experiences blended with "learning by doing" (see discovery learning). Outdoor education is focused on what happens outside of buildings "for the purpose of developing knowledge, skills, and attitudes concerning the world in which we live" (Ford, 1986, p. 3). Hands-on learning (see also) through direct participation is common in outdoor education and may be independent on the part of the learner or teacher-mediated.

Outdoor education has four dimensions: extension, development, content, and teaching methodology. The first dimension, *extension*, consists of knowledge of and concern for the environment that extends formal learning activities beyond the classroom into the community, natural environment, or other locations related to the topics being studied. Ford (1986) suggests that we teach that humans have a responsibility for stewardship or care of the land, facts and concepts regarding the interrelationships of all ecosystems to improve literacy, how to make sound decisions based on scientific facts, how to live comfortably outdoors, how to recreate leisurely in the outdoors with minimal impact on the environment, and how to be life-long learners of outdoor education and to know that outdoor education is a continual education experience.

The second dimension, *development*, focuses on personal growth through problem-solving (see also), challenge and adventure. The third dimension, *content*, emphasizes teaching the traditional subject matter related to the out-of-doors such as ecology, biology, environmental awareness, skills used in the outdoors, and human relationships (Bunting, 2006; Ford, 1986). The final, *teaching methodology*, refers to instruction using teaching tools that enable students to make connections between their outdoor experiences and learning activities such as reflective discussion and journaling (see science notebook) (Bunting, 2006). (LW)

Broda, H. W. (2007). *Schoolyard-enhanced learning*. Portland, Maine: Stenhouse Publishers.

Bunting, C. J. (2006). *Interdisciplinary teaching through outdoor education*. Champaign, IL: Human Kinetics.

Ford, P. (1986). *Outdoor education: Definition and philosophy*. Washington, DC: Office of Educational Research and Improvement.

Hammerman, D. R. (1978). *Historical background of outdoor education*. Taft Campus occasional paper No. 17. Northern Illinois University.

Priest, S. (1986). Redefining outdoor education: A matter of many relationship. *Journal of Environmental Education, 17*(3), 13-15.

Pedagogical Content Knowledge (PCK) refers to what teachers know about how to teach a particular subject or topic (such as balancing chemical reactions) to a particular group of students. PCK is more than general knowledge of teaching and content knowledge of a particular subject.

Lee Shulman (1986) who proposed the concept of PCK, describes it as teachers' understanding of "the most useful forms of representation of the most powerful analogies, illustrations, examples, explanations, and demonstrations – in a word, the ways of representing and formulating the subject ... that make it comprehensible to others" (p. 9).

PCK stands at the intersection of knowledge of content and pedagogy. Teachers with strong PCK ask "What shall I do to help my students understand this science concept," and "What are my students likely to already know about it; "What will be difficult for them" and "What materials and tools do I have available to help foster student understanding" (Gess-Newsome & Lederman, 1999, p. 95).

According to Magnusson and colleagues (1999) and Van Dijk and Kattmann (2007) the most highly developed level of PCK involves knowledge of:

1) The subject matter (i.e. knowledge of content),
2) Students and their conceptions, misconceptions and specific learning difficulties within a given subject or science topic,
3) The curriculum and where the content is best suited for inclusion,
4) The most appropriate content-specific assessment tools,
5) The most effective instructional strategies (including examples, anecdotes, illustrations and related resources) for teaching the science content and
6) General teaching methods

PCK develops from teachers' knowledge of the content, experiences gained during teaching, experience from professional development, and memories of their own experiences as students (Van Dijk & Kattmann, 2007). In other words, it is very difficult to share PCK from one person to another; educators must gain such knowledge as they mature as teachers. This explains why more experienced teachers are likely to be more effective than novice teachers. (PW)

Gess-Newsome, J., & Lederman, N. (1999). *Examining pedagogical content knowledge: The construct and its implications for science education.* Boston, MA: Kluwer.
Magnusson, S., Krajcik, J. S., & Borko, H. (1996). Nature, sources and development of pedagogical content knowledge for science teaching. In J. Gess-Newsome & N. Lederman (Eds.), *Science teacher's knowledge base: The 1994 Association for the Education of Teachers in Science Yearbook.* Washington DC: Association for the Education of Teachers in Science.
Shulman, L. S. (1986). Those who understand: Knowledge growth in teaching. *Educational Researcher, 15*(2), 4-14.
Van Dijk, E. M. & Kattmann, U. (2007). A research model for the study of science teachers' PCK and improving teacher education. *Teaching and Teacher Education, 23*(6), 885-897.

Pedagogical Practices in Science Teaching are any approach or teaching technique an educator chooses to use in the classroom by which they attempt to teach students. The key is for the teacher to use the pedagogical practice and the most appropriate teacher behaviors (Clough, Berg, & Olson, 2009) most likely to increase understanding on the part of the students.

Different pedagogical practices will naturally result in different responses from students. Therefore, first understanding the goals and motivation for the teaching any subject is an important first step to choosing the most appropriate pedagogical practice. An example of the process for choosing an approach may be illustrated in instruction about the concept of gravity. Students newly introduced to this concept could gain understanding from the teacher through being presented a description of an object falling, a visualization of an object falling, and/or physically dropping an object themselves. Each pedagogical process helps to build understanding of the concept in the minds of the students. It often takes a combination of several pedagogical practices to build complete understanding.

An important consideration for selecting a pedagogical practice relates to pedagogical content knowledge (PCK) (see also). PCK "reflects an individual's abilities at effectively communicating content knowledge to others in ways that are understandable" (Patel & Herick, 2010). Teachers with the highest levels of PCK are the ones who will most likely use the most effective pedagogical practices. In other words, effective teachers know what practices work and they apply such practices in a deliberate fashion based on the goals of the lesson and the learning context. These practices might include modeling (e.g. Concept Map – *see also)*, hands-on practice, and laboratory experiments (Shulman, 1987). In addition such practices may also include knowledge of the learning styles of students, students' personal experiences and prior knowledge (Haggis, 2006; Zohar, 2004).

The pedagogical practices used should provide the most effective environments for learning. The most successful teachers will constantly consider which teaching practices or pedagogical practices works best in the classroom. (JK)

Clough, M. P., Berg, C. A., & Olson, J. K. (2009). Promoting effective science teacher education and science teaching: A framework for teacher decision-making. *International Journal of Science and Mathematics Education, 7*(4), 821-847.

Haggis, T. (2006). Pedagogies for diversity: Retaining critical challenge amidst fears of 'dumbing down.' *Studies in Higher Education, 31*(5), 521-535.

Patel, N. H. (2010). Collaborating in higher education: Improving pedagogical practice. *Scholarly Partnerships Education, 5*(2), 7.

Shulman, L. (1987). Knowledge and teaching: Foundations of the new reform. *Harvard Educational Review, 57,* 1-22.

Zohar, A. (2004). Elements of teachers' pedagogical knowledge regarding instruction of higher order thinking. *Journal of Learning Disabilities, 30*(4), 395-407.

Place-based Learning (sometimes referred to as community-based learning) is an instructional approach that promotes learning rooted in a specific locale and involves students in solving community problems or is tied to experiences that are connected to a specific location.

Place-based learning grew out of environmental education and requires students to understand the local community (its unique history, environment, culture, problems, economy, etc.) on a deeper level. This could include the students' own school, neighborhood, town, community, or region (Sobel, 2003). The basic philosophy of place-based learning is to promote students' "sense of place" and provides a grounding connection to that location, before branching out to more complex national or global issues.

Place-based learning often incorporates problem-based or hands-on learning approaches to understand the local environment, community, its history, and the people who inhabit it. Learning about a specific place fosters authentic learning, makes learning relevant, fosters a sense of personal connection, and allows students to better understand their place in society (Smith, 2002).

Place-based learning is interdisciplinary, spanning all academic subjects. In addition to academics, place-based learning promotes responsible citizenship by engaging students in the community and the community in the education of its students (Smith & Sobel, 2010).

Place-based learning (even without using this label) has been used by educators for generations who provide local examples of the topic of study (usually though news reports of current events) to students so they can see the personal relevance of school science. Occasionally such examples may present themselves fortuitously as a "teachable moment" or are actively sought out by teachers.

An example of place-based learning would be to have students near the Gulf coast in the U.S. study the oil spill that occurred in April of 2010. Links to school science could be made through an investigation of the impact of the oil spill on water quality and marine ecosystems. Community-based problems worthy of consideration could include the loss of income from fishing and shrimping, effects on the local economy, the clean-up, and the way it affected the lives of people living in the Gulf coast region. (CW)

Smith, G. (2002). Place-based education: Learning to be where we are. *Phi Delta Kappan,* *83*(8), 584-594.

Smith, G. A., & Sobel, D. (2010). *Place- and community-based education in schools.* New York, NY: Routledge.

Sobel, D. (2003). *Place-based education.* Great Barrington, MA: The Orion Society.

Prior Knowledge relates to the pre-existing information (Bransford et al., 2000) or prior understandings (Donovan & Bransford, 2005) held by students before instruction begins. Such prior knowledge consists of accurate perceptions along with misconceptions (see also) and alternative conceptions. Prior knowledge can either support or interfere with future understanding.

Bransford and colleagues (2000) call prior knowledge what an individual student "brings to the classroom, based on their personal and idiosyncratic experiences ..." (p. 71). With respect to science, students will often have some information about a subject or some conception of how things work. Don't elementary students know much more about dinosaurs than most teachers? Therefore, what students already know will be tied to the learning and the accommodation of new information. They explain further that prior knowledge is "not only a generic set of experiences attributable to developmental stages through which learners may have passed ... [it] ... also includes the kind of knowledge that learners acquire because of their social roles, such as those connected with race, class, gender and their culture and ethnic affiliations ..." (pp. 71-72).

Prior knowledge is an important part of constructivist or conceptual change teaching (see also). This idea about how people learn is based on an expectation that individuals will likely have some advance knowledge and this knowledge plays a role in what is learned next and how future learning is processed by the learner. Therefore, it is vital that science teachers recognize the prior knowledge held by their students so that they can design lessons to support such knowledge if it is correct or replace such knowledge if it is not. Students too must have opportunities to explore what they already know so that they can consider this knowledge and compare it to the lessons taught in school science class.

That students recognize what they already know is important because prior experiences and information influence future learning. This creates a scheme that assists the individual in "comprehending new information, ... [and] serve as a guide for goal-directed activities ..., and fill in gaps in information ... (Gredler, 2009, p. 200). Thinking about ones thinking (see also metacognition) will help the learner in determining if prior knowledge is correct in its original conception. Paying attention to what one already knows can help the learner take control of future learning (Donovan & Bransford, 2005) by monitoring understanding (Gredler, 2009). When the learner recognizes that their prior knowledge does not match what is being taught, students may more likely ask questions, read the textbook more deeply and pay closer attention in class. (JH)

Bransford, J. D., Brown, A. L., & Cocking, R. R. (Eds.). (2000). *How people learn: Brain, mind experience and school.* Committee on Developments in the Science of Learning. Division of Behavioral and Social Sciences and Education of the National Research Council. Washington, DC: National Academies Press.

Donovan, M. S., & Bransford, J. D. (2005). Introduction. In M. S. Donovan & J. D. Bransford (Eds.), *How students learn: Science in the classroom* (pp. 1-26). Washington, DC: National Academies Press.

Gredler, M. E. (2009). *Learning and instruction: Theory into practice* (6th ed.). Upper Saddle River: Pearson.

Probes and Probeware facilitate the collection and management of data in science, math and technology classes and are often used in tandem with Microcomputer Based Labs (see also). The probes are digital sensors that measure a variety of factors including temperature, pH, dissolved oxygen, pressure and many other variables. The probeware is best defined as the software residing on the computer that drives the probes, captures and displays data but many use the terms interchangeably.

Some of the primary foundations of science include investigations, exploration, asking questions, analyzing, and thinking. The use of computers attached to various data capture devises (called probes) provides a unique opportunity that supports observation and inquiry that is typically lacking in many elementary science programs (Linn, 2003; Zuker et al., 2007). There are several manufacturers of probes and most produce devices that can capture data related to pressure, temperature, sound, light, motion, etc. The related software can be set up on a tablet or laptop computer or handheld "data logger" to record data at a particular rate and show the resulting graph of these data directly on a screen.

According to Metcalf and Tinker (2004), although science standards call for the increased use of technology, this is often missing in actual classroom practice. Probes and probeware can be an easy and cost effective way to provide student opportunities to engage in data collection and analysis, understanding changes, integration with mathematics, student-led investigations, and modeling.

In a meta-analysis of 42 studies of computer-assisted instruction (CAI) in science education yielding 108 effect sizes, Bayraktar (2001) found an overall effect size of 0.27 standard deviations. This means that a "typical student" using CAI moved from the 50th percentile to the 62nd percentile in science. Also Bayraktar found that simulations and tutorials in science were significantly more effective than drill-and-practice techniques.

Probes and software can be used by students to collect data in an attempt to explore and explain science phenomena. For example two students may use two force probes connected together by a rubber band to investigate what happens to the force graphs when each of the students applies different forces to the rubberband. A temperature probe can be used to measure what happens when a cup of hot water is mixed with a cup of cold water. Is the temperature of the mixed water exactly in the middle of the temperature of the hot and cold cups? Such an investigation can be run dozens of times using probes with the data for each trial stored and visualized on the computer with the related probeware. (CB)

Bayraktar, S. (2001) A meta-analysis of the effectiveness of computer assisted instruction in science education. *Journal of Research in Technology Education, 34*(2), 173-188.

Linn, M. C. (2003) Technology and science education: Starting points, research programs, and trends. *International Journal of Science Education, 25*(6), 727-758.

Metcalf, S. J., & Tinker, R. F. (2004). Probeware and handhelds in elementary and middle school science. *Journal of Science Education and Technology, 13*(1), 43-49.

Zucker, A. A., Tinker, R., Staudt, C., Mansfield, A., & Metalf, S. (2007). Learning science in grades 3-8 using probeware and computers: Findings from the TEEMSS II project. *Journal of Science Education Technology, 17*(1), 42-48.

Problem Based Learning is an inquiry (see also) teaching strategy related to project based instruction (see also) in which students are given real-world situations or scenarios ("problems") and asked to offer insights regarding or solutions. Typically the "teacher presents students with an authentic, ill-structured problem *before* they receive any instruction" (Grabinger et al., 1995, p. 8).

Problem-based (and case-based) learning began in the 1960's in medical schools and expanded to business, legal and engineering education. Problem-based and project-based (see also) modes of teaching are similar. The problem provides an opportunity for contextualized learning; proposed solutions (or explanations) are offered, discussed and defended through deep learning experiences. However, there is no product developed as is the case in project-based instruction (see also).

Prince and Felder (2007) state that problem-based learning works bests when "students – usually working in teams – are confronted with an ill-structured open-ended real-world problem to solve, and take the lead in defining the problem precisely, figuring out what they know and what they need to determine, and how to proceed to determine it. They formulate and evaluate alternative solutions, select the best one and make a case for it, and evaluate lessons learned" (p. 15).

In an example, (with a role playing component) from the American Chemical Society (2006) students learn about the properties of water, solubility, and pH by investigating the causes of a "fish-kill." With data supplied by the teacher, student groups examine the issue from various perspectives (town council, power company officials, etc.). Arguments are made and questions asked and the town council group offers a decision on the cause of the problem.

Prince and Felder (2007) point out the pros and cons of problem based learning. First, students may be more motivated to learn supporting concepts, facts and principles because these elements are linked to the solution to the problem. Also, because problem-based challenges are ideally set in "messy" real world situations, students learn content and even overarching principles of the discipline in a contextualized fashion. They report increases in "students' skills development, retention of knowledge, and ability to apply learned materials, but it does not have a statistically significant effect on academic achievement" (pp. 15-16). Conversely, problem-based learning may be hard to implement. It is time consuming to develop appropriate and open-ended problems that still facilitate learning the desired content. They recommend that instructors look for problems that have already been developed rather than producing new ones immediately. (WM/JH)

Note, there is much overlap between project and problem based instruction and both are frequently called PBL. To reinforce the distinction, it would be useful to refer to Problem-based Learning as PBL and the newer, Project-based Instruction as PBI or Project-based Science as PBS. Doing so would eliminate much confusion presently found in the literature.

American Chemical Society. (2006). *Chemistry in the community.* New York: W. H. Freeman.

Grabiner, S., Dunlap, J. C., & Duffield, J. A. (1995). Rich environments for active learning in action: Problem-based learning. *Assn. for Learning Technology Journal, 3*(2), 5-34.

Prince, M., & Felder, R. (2007). The many faces of inductive teaching and learning. *Journal of College Science Teaching, 35*(5), 14-20.

Problem Solving is a cognitive process that occurs when individuals are engaged in the resolution of a complex issue (i.e. the problem) (Sunal & Sunal, 2003). In classroom use, students typically are asked to apply what they have learned by using new knowledge and skills to address problems given to them, thus they have opportunities to practice the skills necessary to understand, investigate, and attempt to determine a solution to some question.

One of the difficulties of the term "problem" is that what could be a problem, issue, or concern for one individual may not be an issue for another. The National Council of Teachers of Mathematics (2000) reminds us that problem solving is working through a solution that is not known beforehand. Therefore, the best problems used in problem-solving activities are those that all students would find puzzling and intriguing. When this occurs students can apply thinking strategies "directed at achieving a goal when a solution method is not obvious to the problem solver" (Mayer & Wittrock, 1996, p. 47). Ultimately, the pedagogical practice (see also) called "problem solving" relates to having students apply what they have previously learned to something new.

There is no single teaching method known as problem solving, but problem solving refers to the idea that students can learn more effectively by applying what they have learned rather than simply repeating what the teacher or textbooks have said. Problem solving is the main activity in a teaching technique called Problem Based Learning (PBL) in which students are presented problems, often developed from the real world, and asked to suggest solutions for those problems.

Ernst (2009) tells us that when teachers use problem solving in the classroom students engage in instructional activities that are not directly taught. Students learn by experiencing general processes that stimulate and engage them in developing abilities to solve diverse challenges.

In the science classroom, students might learn about how a pendulum operates by exploring the properties of a pendulum (length of the string and the size of the object hanging from it). Then the students would be asked to solve a problem related to the pendulum such as how long should the string be in order for the pendulum to swing back and forth once every second. A student could solve this problem only if they really understand that the length of the string and the force of gravity impact pendulum motion not the mass of the object or the amount by which the object is pulled back before it is let go. (SI)

Ernst, J. V. (2009). Contextual problem solving model origination. *Journal of Industrial Teacher Education. 46*(2), 27-47.

Mayer, R. E., & Wittrock, M. C. (1996). Problem-solving transfer. In D. C. Berliner & R. C. Calfee (Eds.), *Handbook of educational psychology* (pp. 4-62). New York: Simon & Schuster Macmillan.

National Council of Teachers of Mathematics. (2000). *Principles and standards for school mathematics*. Reston, VA: The National Council of Teachers of Mathematics.

Sunal, D. W., & Sunal, C. S. (2003). *Science in the elementary and middle school*. Upper Saddle River, NJ: Merrill Prentice Hall.

Process Orientated Guided Instruction (POGIL) is an instructional approach much like the learning cycle (see also) in which students work in small groups engaging in specially designed activities while the instructor acts as a facilitator. "The POGIL approach has two broad aims: to develop mastery through student construction of understanding, and to develop and improve important learning skills such as information processing, oral and written communication, critical thinking, problem solving, and metacognition and assessment" (Moog & Spencer, 2008, p. 3).

The POGIL method combines two prominent education philosophies: cooperative learning and the learning cycle (see also). According to Moog et al.(2008), when students construct understanding, discuss and debate various ideas, and share different ideas and understandings within a group setting, their individual performance improves.

One learning cycle approach recommended by advocates of POGIL has three phases. (1) In the "exploration," students review patterns in the data or the environment in which they generate hypotheses and then test those hypotheses to better understand the information. (2) In the "Term Introduction" phase, students develop a concept from the patterns in the data. By having this phase follow the "exploration" phase, students are introduced to a new term after already constructing an understanding of the concept. In the traditional lecture setting, students are introduced to the term first and then presented with examples. Finally (3) in the "application" phase, students use the newly developed concept in a new situation in order to generalize the concept's meaning and applicability (Bailey, Minderhout, and Loertscher, 2012; Moog & Spencer, 2008).

In a chemistry POGIL activity addressing the components of an atom, students are given a series of diagrams or examples of different atoms and ions that includes the number and location of the protons, neutrons, and elections. The teacher serving as the facilitator asks a series of guiding questions (see also) that lead students to recognize that the number of protons identifies each element. At this point the teacher introduces the term "atomic number" and students "apply" this concept to other elements on the periodic table. (Moog & Spencer, 2008). (CB)

Bailey, C. P., Minderhout, V., & Loertscher, J. (2012). Learning transferable skills in large lecture halls: Implementing a POGIL approach in biochemistry. *Biochemistry and Molecular Biology Education, 40*(1), 1-7.

Moog, R. S., & Spencer, J. N. (2008). POGIL: An overview. In Moog et al. (Eds.), *Process Oriented Guided Inquiry Learning (POGIL)* (pp. 1-13). Washington DC: American Chemical Society.

Programme for International Student Assessment **(PISA)** is an international assessment launched by the Organisation for Economic Co-operation and Development (OECD) that measures the mathematics, reading, and science literacy of 15-year-olds (NCES, 2013; OECD, 2013).

Since the assessment program began in 1997, over 70 countries have participated at least once. Every three years, a randomly selected group of 15-year-old students take the test, which primarily focuses on one key subject. In 2000, PISA focused on reading, in 2003 mathematics and problem solving, in 2006 science literacy, in 2009 reading, and in 2012 mathematics with an optional computer-based assessment of mathematics and reading and financial literacy. Thirty countries added the optional assessment in mathematics and reading while only 19 countries added the optional financial literacy assessment. Science will not be the primary focus again until 2015.

Unlike state-level assessments, PISA does not directly measure school curriculum, and therefore, uses student background questionnaires to help analysts interpret PISA results. The PISA assessments "are designed to assess to what extent students at the end of compulsory education, can apply their knowledge to real-life situations and be equipped for full participation in society" (OECD, 2013, p. 1)

As an example of PISA results, consider these for the United States from the 2009 assessment. For science literacy, the average score of U.S. 15-year-olds was 502, which was not significantly different from the OECD average of 501. Of the 33 OECD countries who tested, 12 had higher average scores than the United States: Finland (554), Japan (539), Korea (535), New Zealand (532), Canada (529), Estonia (528), Australia (527), the Netherlands (522), Germany (520), Switzerland (517), the United Kingdom (514), and Slovenia (512). 12 OECD countries had average scores not measurably different and 9 countries had lower average scores. In 2006, United States students average science literacy score was 489 but was a 491 in 2003 (NCES, 2013; OECD, 2009). (CB)

National Center for Education Statistics (2013). Program for international student assessment (PISA). Washington, DC: Author. Retrieved from
http://nces.ed.gov/surveys/pisa/index.asp
Organisation for Economic Co-operation and Development. (2013). OECD programme for international student assessment (PISA). Paris, France: Author. Retrieved from
http://www.oecd.org/pisa/aboutpisa/ http://www.oecd.org/pisa/aboutpisa/
Organisation for Economic Co-operation and Development (2009). Figure 1: Comparing countries' and economies' performance. Paris, France: Author. Retrieved from
http://www.oecd.org/pisa/46643496.pdf

Project 2061 is a "long terms initiative" of the American Association for the Advancement of Science (AAAS) "to help all Americans become literate in science, mathematics, and technology," (AAAS, 2013) There are many related projects associated with this goal including development of standards, learning progressions and assessment tools.

Project 2061's areas of expertise include developing learning goals and curriculum, creating online assessments of students' misconceptions, and improving student achievement through teacher development. Those working for this initiative have produced a host of print and online resources, tools, and research for teachers, families, and communities, as well as workshops and conferences for educators.

Project 2061 began in 1985, the most recent year in which Halley's Comet was visible. The project derives its name from the year that the comet will again return The name serves to remind us that we are preparing children now are very likely be alive to see the return of the comet for a changing world full of scientific innovation and technology. To that end, Project 2061 is pursuing five major areas of research and development: learning goals, curriculum materials, teaching and learning, testing and assessment, and family and community.

First, *Project 2061* has produced a collection of materials on learning goals intended to guide the development of curriculum materials, research, testing, as well as resources for families and communities. For example, their *Benchmarks for Science Literacy* published in 1993 (see also) have influenced learning goals at the state and local levels in math, science, and technology. The *Atlas of Science Literacy* (see also) published in 2001 and 2007, show "maps" of K-12 learning goals as they relate to each other and how learning progresses from grade to grade.

For the second area of research and development, Project 2061 has published evaluations of textbooks and curricular materials for high school biology, middle school science, algebra, and middle school mathematics. Toward their third goal of improving teaching and learning, Project 2061 is engaged in two major research projects that will contribute to teachers' understandings of science and math teaching and learning: studying how to provide professional development and continued support for teachers to help improve student learning of key ideas and skills in middle school math as well as implementing new graduate and postdoctoral programs in curriculum materials development which will conduct research on design and use of effective curriculum materials for science learning.

Project 2061 has done extensive work toward their fourth goal, testing and assessment, by creating an online assessment site for educators. Those involved developed the assessment items and collected data with a grant from NSF and to help teachers assess what students do and don't know about science. Finally, in the area of family and community, Project 2061 has created resources to empower families to improve their child's science education, including science websites for kids, a family guide to science, and articles for parents on science education. (AB)

American Association for the Advancement of Science. (2013). *Programs: Education.* Retrieved from http://www.project2061.org/default.htm

Project-based Instruction is a type of inquiry teaching (see also) related to problem-based instruction (see also) in which students are given real-world challenges, situations or scenarios and asked to address these challenges and – generally – produce a product as a solution not just offer a proposed response.

Project-based instruction is an extension of problem-based learning (see also) but Capraro and Slough (2013) emphasize that they two are not the same. "Project based learning is broader and often is composed of several problems student will need to solve" and "provides the contextualized, authentic experiences necessary for students to scaffold learning and build meaningfully powerful science, technology, engineering, and mathematics concepts" (p. 2) supported by other school disciplines. Project-based instruction can play an important role in integrated STEM programs because the projects typically demand that students use content, techniques and conclusions from all four of the STEM disciplines.

Thomas (2000) states that the projects must be a) central to the curriculum, b) focused on driving questions, c) involve students in constructive investigation, d) are student driven, and e) are related to real life. Collaboration is considered a final element. Prince and Felder (2007) add that students must produce some artifact "such as a process or product design, computer code or simulation, or the design of an experiment and the analysis and interpretation of the data" (p. 16).

A summary of research (Thomas, 2000) shows that with project based approaches there are positive impacts on students' content knowledge, engagement, critical thinking, problem solving, and collaborative skills. Teachers report problems with implementation, time and classroom management, and assessment. Resources are available to support project based learning such as those from the Buck Institute (Markham, et al., 2003) which provides advice for planning, crafting the driving question, assessment, along with sample projects. Krajcik, McNeill and Reiser (2007) have developed a model called IQWST to support project-based instruction. (WM)

Note, there is much overlap between project and problem based instruction and both are frequently called PBL. To reinforce the distinction, it would be useful to refer to Problem-based Learning as PBL and the newer, Project-based Instruction as PBI or Project-based Science as PBS. Doing so would eliminate much confusion presently found in the literature.

Capraro, R.M. and Slough, S.W. (2009). Why PBL? Why STEM? Why now? (pp.1-5). In R. M. Capraro, M. M. Capraro, & J. R. Morgan (Eds.), *STEM Project Based Learning.* Boston: Sense Publishers.

Krajcik, J., McNeill, K. L., & Reiser, B. J. (2007). Learning-goals-driver design model: Developing curriculum materials that align with national standards and incorporate project-based pedagogy. *Science Education, 92*(1), 1-32.

Markham, T., Larmer, J., & Ravitz, J. (2003). *Project based learning handbook: A guide to standards-focused project based learning.* Novato, CA: Buck Institute for Education.

Prince, M., & Felder, R. (2007). The many faces of inductive teaching and learning. *Journal of College Science Teaching, 35*(5), 14-20.

Thomas, J. W. (2000). *A review of research on project-based learning.* Report prepared for The Autodesk Foundation. Retrieved June 3, 2013 from http://www.bie.org/index.php/site/RE/pbl_research/29

Questioning Strategies are those question-asking forms and tools used by teachers to help students review material, to fuel critical thinking, to reduce disruptive behavior, to enhance creativity, to check for understanding, to regulate classroom activities, to determine student grades, to foster discussion, to reduce inattentiveness, and for many other reasons (Blosser, 1991). There are many strategies and techniques associated with questioning including the use of Socratic dialogues, wait time and higher/lower level questioning.

Often times, teachers are so used to asking questions that they fail to analyze why or how they do it. According to Blosser (1991), questions need to do more than determine if a student does or does not understand a particular concept. About 60 percent of teacher questions recall only facts while 20 percent require students to think and another 20 percent are procedural.

Guided questions can generally be divided into 7 categories or less based on Blooms Taxonomy: (1) memory or recall (2) translation or rephrasing using different language or symbols, (3) interpretation or finding relationships, (4) application or solving real-life problems through generalizations, (5) analysis or solving a problem through critical thinking, (6) synthesis or solving a problem using creative thinking, and (7) evaluation or making judgments using standards or rules (Blosser, 1991).

A teacher can determine what type of questions he or she most often asks by determining the number of possible responses, examining whether the question requires students to utilize past information when framing a response, and analyzing specific words or phrases in the question. For example, *who, what, when, where,* and *why* usually mean the question is closed while terms such as *compare, interpret, explain,* or *evaluate* may require more than pulling from memorized information. Teaches should watch the length of the question so that it is not too vague or too wordy. One important questioning skill is to ask a variety of questions particularly open questions where the teacher may ask for examples, for clarification of an idea, for a longer and more in-depth explanation. Lastly, teachers should provide students with a silent moment or "wait time" lasting about three to five seconds after asking a question, so students have an opportunity to formulate a response (Blosser, 1991; Elstgeest, 1985; Rowe, 1986) (CB/WM).

Blosser, P. E. (1991). *How to ask the right questions.* Washington, DC: National Science Teachers Association.
Elstgeest, J. (1985). The right question at the right time. From W. Harlen (Ed.), *Primary science: Taking the plunge* (pp. 36-45). Heinemann Educational Books.
Rowe, M. B. (1986, Jan-Feb). Wait time: Slowing down may be a way of speeding up! *Journal of Teacher Education, 37*(1), 43-50.

Reasoning is the process by which an individual consciously tries to make sense of experiences, objects, and interactions, establishing and verifying information, and altering or justifying beliefs, practices, and institutions based on new experiences and information (Kompridis, 2000).

For more than 50 years, science educators have emphasized the need for the inclusion of argumentation (see also) and evidence-based reasoning in science classrooms. More recent efforts have pushed for instruction and classroom activities to mirror the scientific activities and thinking process of scientists and for evidence-based reasoning to become "the core of students' experiences in science classrooms" (Brown et al., 2010, p. 125). The American Association for the Advancement of Science (1993) and National Research Council (1996, 2001, 2007) recommend that science learning environments develop and enhance students' abilities to reason using evidence and argumentation.

In order for students to debate and discuss scientific ideas, they must know how to use and evaluate evidence, and "the use or misuse of supporting evidence, the language used, and the logic of the argument presented are important considerations in judging how seriously to take an assertion or hypothesis" (Brown et al., 2010, p. 124). "The ability to reason from evidence, along with understanding the central role evidence plays in science, is a core element in the development of scientifically literate students" (p. 125). (CB)

American Association for the Advancement of Science. (1993). *Benchmarks for science literacy.* New York: Oxford University Press.

Brown, N. J. S., Furtak, E. M., Timms, M. Nagashima, S. O., & Wilson, M. (2010). The evidence-based reasoning framework: Assessing scientific reasoning. *Educational Assessment, 15*(3/5), 123-141.

Kompridis, N. (2000). So we need something else for reason to mean. *International Journal of Philosophical Studies, 8*(3), 271-295.

National Research Council. (1996). *National science education standards.* Washington, DC: National Academy Press.

National Research Council. (2001). *Knowing what students know: The science and design of educational assessment.* Washington, DC: National Academy Press.

National Research Council. (2007). *Taking science to school: Learning and teaching science in grades K-8.* Washington, DC: National Academy Press.

Scaffolding is a teaching technique by which educators provide relevant support to a student learning to master a task or a problem in much the way that a building is constructed, one floor at a time. Teachers provide just enough help, ask appropriate questions, provide relevant examples that students are able to learn necessary concepts and build higher level of understanding.

The term *scaffolding* in education is like the temporary structure built to support and provides safety for construction workers. Teachers who use scaffolding help students make connections among the concepts and knowledge they already have, while creating safe and effective learning environment for students. They do this by simplifying the elements of the problem that are too difficult for the child to complete at that time, with the expectation that the child will eventually be able to complete all task elements. The teacher encourages the child to participate meaningfully in the activity by maintaining enough of a challenge for the child to stay interested, by determining where the learner needs assistance and asks questions to assist the student in making the desired connections.

Educators who scaffold build on what students know and extend their capabilities by providing support structures for the student's performance of a task or skill (Bransford, 2000). Although the idea emphasizing the critical role of adults in guiding and supporting students' learning stems from the work of Russian psychologist Lev Vygotsky, researcher Jerome Bruner and associates brought the term scaffolding to light in the United States.

Bruner's team (Wood, Bruner, & Ross, 1976) determined six important elements of the scaffolding process: 1) *Recruitment* of the child's interest in a task; 2) *Demonstrating solutions* to the problem; 3) *Simplifying the task*; 4) *Maintaining participation* of the child through encouragement and a focus on the goal; 5) *Providing feedback* to the child about the difference between what he or she is doing and what is needed to complete the task; and 6) *Controlling frustration* and risk levels of the child while he or she is finding problem solutions (Meece, 1997).

In the science classroom, a teacher may use scaffolding when demonstrating lab skills, leading students through the steps of a complicated stoichiometry or physics problem, breaking a complex investigation into smaller tasks, doing part of a conversion problem as a group, asking questions to help students find their own errors, and providing detailed feedback on students' work. Science teachers may also provide strategies that help students become better science writers (using templates, sentence-starters, and writing prompts). For example, to help students write evidence-based conclusions, an instructor might model writing a conclusion for a laboratory report first with the whole class, then scale back the support provided to students each time they attempt this skill in the future. (AB)

Bransford, J. (2000). *How people learn: Brain, mind, experience, and school*. Washington, DC: National Academy Press.

Meece, J. L. (1997). *Child and adolescent development for educators*. NY: McGraw-Hill.

Wood, D., Bruner, J. S., & Ross, G. (1976). The role of tutoring in problem solving. *Journal of Child Psychology and Psychiatry, 17*(2), 89-100.

Science and Engineering Practices comprise the first dimension of three found in the Next Generation Science Standards (NGSS) published in 2013 and *A Framework for K-12 Science Education* published in 2012.

These practices are derived from those that scientists and engineers use as part of their professional work. The NGSS describe the practices as "behaviors that scientists engage in as they investigate and build models and theories about the natural world and the key set of engineering practices that engineers use as they design and build models and systems" (Achieve, 2013).

The 8 practices, in the *Framework for K-12 Science Education* (National Research Council, 2012), are:

1. Asking questions (for science) and defining problems (for engineering);
2. Developing and using models;
3. Planning and carrying out investigations;
4. Analyzing and interpreting data;
5. Using mathematics and computational thinking;
6. Constructing explanations (for science) and designing solutions (for engineering);
7. Engaging in argument from evidence; and
8. Obtaining, evaluating, and communicating information (pp. 42, 49).

The *Framework* discusses each of the practices in depth, including the major competencies each student should have before graduating and how students' competence should progress across grade levels. These same practices are included in the NGSS with the intention that all science students will engage in and experience them, not just learn about them. Like the crosscutting concepts, the scientific and engineering practices are designed so that students understand that science is not an isolated body of facts but a connected web of ideas and skills. Likewise, students learn of the relationships between science and engineering and what distinguishes these two fields from each other.

This is an important issue because students might confuse the two by studying them together. Therefore, when introducing students to the practices, teachers must differentiate between scientific inquiry and engineering design, since there are differences in the work of these two fields. Teachers must emphasize the cognitive, social, and physical practices that scientists engage in and that engineers apply. The teaching of scientific procedures should not be devoid of content and should not promote just one linear scientific method. By having students enact these practices throughout their school career, teachers can help students overcome a naïve conception of how work in science and engineering are done and how related scientific knowledge develops (National Research Council, 2012). (AB)

Achieve, Inc. (2013). *The Next Generation Science Standards: Three dimensions.* Washington, DC: Author. Retrieved from http://www.nextgenscience.org/three-dimensions.

National Research Council (US). (2011). *A framework for K-12 science education: Practices, crosscutting concepts, and core ideas.* Washington, DC: National Academies Press.

Science Education is the scholarly and practical discipline concerned with the teaching, learning and assessment of science content, science processes and the nature of science. Science educators conduct research to address problems in science teaching and learning, develops policy statements, engage in informed political debate regarding the place of science instruction in schools and in society, educate future science teachers, and assess the state of science knowledge and understanding.

Unfortunately, there is no widely shared definition of science education, but to develop one it will be useful to consider the work of the scientist, science teacher, and science educator, all of whom make important but somewhat distinct contributions.

Scientists explore and attempt to understand the natural world, and then communicate this new knowledge to other scientists. Science teachers are responsible for knowing the content, nature and processes of science and effectively communicating such knowledge to students. Science educators have characteristics of both scientists and science teachers. Science education is a unique and valuable discipline that extends beyond the generation of new scientific knowledge and effective classroom presentation of that knowledge.

Like many disciplines, defining science education is best accomplished by examining the work done by those identifying themselves as part of that discipline and in doing so establish the following list of job skills and attributes. Science educators should deeply understand research-based science teaching practices, be master teachers of science content, assist teachers and schools in improving science instruction, and also be engaged in research to improve teaching and learning of science. Science educators will also understand the history of the discipline of science education, know and help to develop effective curriculum models and other tools to support science teaching, and aid in the preparation of new science teachers. Science educators will understand and react to educational and social trends with respect to science instruction and will write policies and engage in political action to support high quality science instruction and science communication in schools, museums, media, and elsewhere. Many of those with the title "science educator" are employed as curriculum designers, researchers, and teacher educators in universities or as program officers and administrators within government agencies.

Even though science teaching and learning have been objects of study for more than a century (Bybee, 1977), science education still has some characteristics of an emerging discipline as evidenced by a lack of a shared definition and the absence of formal credentials for entry into the profession. This situation is changing; there are form educational programs that award advanced degrees in "science education," journals, professional societies and a large and growing international group of scholars engaged in research to support the improvement of science teaching and learning who call themselves science educators. (WM/KM)

Bybee, R. (1977). The new transformation of science education. *Science Education, 61*(1), 85-97.

Science Fairs, Exhibitions, and Research Competitions are events where students display information they have gathered from conducting an independent science investigation. They are a science education experience through which students have the opportunity to present the results of an authentic experience in doing science that closely simulates what real world scientists do (McComas, 2011).

Other terms synonymous with science fair include "science exhibition" and "science research competition." A science exhibition could differ from a Science fair in that it may allow models or demonstrations to be presented along with actual experimentation type projects. Generally this term is used in conjunction with science fair. The students are generally judged on the thoroughness of how their work was done and their ability to communicate findings to the judges both orally and visually.

Research competitions may differ from science fairs and exhibitions by asking participants to solve a problem related to a specific topic or theme. For example Toshiba/NSTA ExploraVision (2010) asks students to take a current item of technology and predict how it will change in the future. The International Sustainable World Energy, Engineering and Environment Project (I-SWEEEP (2010), research competition, for example, is focused on projects related to solving challenges related to sustainability. All science fairs are considered by some to be research competitions. All students who participate in a science fair, exhibit or competition ought to be engaged in true inquiry experiences (see also) and learning some valid lessons about the nature of science (see also) (McComas, 2011).

The participants in a science fair may range from elementary age to high school with varying levels of competition. Although some fairs remain only local events, many students will begin at the school site and if successful may move on to compete at increasingly larger fairs, and potentially the International Science Fair. Even if students do not move from the local level, they still will have had a unique and important science learning experience. The International Science and Engineering Fair is sponsored by Intel Corporation and draws participants from more than sixty-five countries and territories and can trace its origins back to 1928 (Society for Science and the Public, 2011). In order to participate in the Intel ISEF, local schools and fairs must follow certain procedures and paperwork designated by Intel ISEF and regulations and experimental procedures that research scientists would follow. (KM)

ExploraVsion, (2010). ExploraVision: Tomorrow's innovation comes from today's young minds. Retrieved from http://www.exploravision.org/

I-SWEEEP, (2010). International Sustainable World Project Olympiad. Houston, TX: Author. Retrieved from http://www.isweeep.org/

McComas, W. (2011). The science fair: A new look at an old tradition. *The Science Teacher, 78*(8), 34-38.

Society for Science & the Public. (2011). Intel International Science and Engineering Fair. Washington, DC: Author. Retrieved from http://www.societyforscience.org/isef

Science Notebooks are journals in which students record their thoughts, questions and observations and related impressions in conjunction with science investigations. Such notebooks are common educational practice (Minogue et al., 2010) in science classes.

"Notebooking" is simply the process of having students record focus questions, materials, procedures, observations, data, drawings, explanations, and/or reflections. Exactly what students' record can be quite open and might even include producing poems and/or drawings. Also, the teacher may provide specific directions about what students should include in their notebooks. Science notebooks help students build and maintain an organized and living document much like scientists do in the laboratory and field.

Students' records in their notebooks should serve as the basis for evidence-based arguments and conclusions they make. The process of notebooking engages children in science learning as well as the writing and communication aspects of the scientific process (Chesbro, 2006). Notebooking also promotes literacy and provides opportunities for students to engage in writing. The specific instructional purpose for writing differs. If students write for the purpose of generating a record of science experiences, for example, notebooks would contain descriptions of what was done, how it was done, and what resulted or what was found (Shepardson & Britsch, 1997). The notebook can also be similar to a traditional laboratory report. Notebook writing that serves as a process through which the students make sense of their investigations begin with a purpose or question followed by the investigative procedure, data collected, and an explanation of findings.

In addition to assisting students with their personal understanding, science notebooks may be used as a formative assessment (see also) tool by the science teacher (Minogue et al., 2010) to determine what students are thinking along with their reasoning. Notebooks can be used by the teacher to promote and evaluate students' conceptual understanding of science concepts, meaning of the investigation and results, proficiencies in the scientific procedures, and writing ability. Students should understand whether their notebooks will be seen by teachers and perhaps shared with classmates or others. What the student writes will depend on their understanding of who will see the notebook in the future and why. (LW)

Chesbro, R. (2006). Using interactive science notebooks for inquiry-based science. *Science Scope, 29*(7), 30-34.

Minogue, J., Madden, L., Bedward, J., Wiebe, E., & Carter, M. (2010). The cross-case analyses of elementary students' engagement in the strands of science proficiency. *Journal of Science Teacher Education, 21*(5), 559-587.

Shephardson, D. P., & Britsch, S. J. (1997). Children's science journals: Tools for teaching, learning and assessing. *Science and Children, 34*(5), 12-17, 46-47.

Science Process Skills are those general procedures that scientists are thought to engage in most of the time (such as measuring, observing, etc.). Many recommend that students should experience these processes in their science instructional experiences.

There are many suggestions for what *science process skills* students should learn and experience, but the most important set of recommendations came in 1967 when a group of science educators and scientists at the American Association for the Advancement of Science (AAAS) studied scientists at work and developed a list of skills that were widely used by all scientists. This idea was to develop a way of teaching science in which science learners would use various tools and procedures to better understand the natural world and to engage in learning about the natural world in the same ways as scientists do.

The list of 12 science process skills was divided between what were called "basic" skills (observing, using space/time relationships, using numbers, inferring, measuring, communicating, classifying and predicting) to be taught first, and the "integrated" science processes skills (controlling variables, defining operationally, formulating hypotheses, interpreting data, and experimenting) to be taught in upper elementary or intermediate grades. Both sets of skills were designed to have the student engage actively with the learning of science and better understand the processes of a scientist (AAAS, 1967).

This set of skills formed the basis for a curriculum project called *Science – A Process Approach* or S-APA. S-APA was created to teach students scientific investigation methods and to provide teachers guidance on which practices students should learn during the elementary years (AAAS, 1967).

The idea that students should learn and engage in some of the processes of science has been an element of science instruction for many years. Most science educators recommend that the students practice such skills while solving real problems rather than simply learning the skills themselves unrelated to real (sometimes called authentic) problem solving (see also authentic science learning contexts and problem based learning).

Finley (1983) argued that S-APA engaged students in science processes without regard for any scientific context and as such was not authentic. There are some who do not feel the designation of science process skills outlining a method promoting inquiry is appropriate. Jadrich and Bruxvoort (2011) and many others agree that teaching "individual process skills divorced from scientific content or contexts" (p. 8) makes little sense in practice. (JH)

American Association for the Advancement of Science (AAAS). (1967). *Science – A process approach.* Washington, DC: AAAS.

Finley, F. (1983). Science processes. *Journal of Research in Science Teaching, 20*(1), 47-54.

Jadrich, J., & Bruxvoort, C. (2011). *Learning and teaching scientific inquiry: Research and Applications.* Arlington, VA: NSTA Press.

Science, Technology, and Society (S/T/S) is frequently defined as a practical and philosophical approach to science instruction that focuses on the use of societal issues as a motivating context to teach relevant traditional science content.

During the late 1970s, educators suggested that one purpose of science teaching is for students to understand the societal impact of science on society and, to a lesser extent, the impact of society on science. Gallagher (1971) and Ziman (1980) are often cited as the founders of this new "society" focus in science instruction. DeBoer (1991) calls science-society teaching as "humanistic, value-oriented and relevant to a wide range of personal, societal and environmental concerns" (pp. 178-179). Early curriculum projects developed in the UK, Netherlands, and Canada focused on the science-society link but typically did not include technology.

By the 1980s, "science and society" had become S/T/S with "technology as a connector between science and society" (Yager, 1996, p. 9). S/T/S was labeled a 'megatrend' by Rustam Roy of the Pennsylvania State University and endorsed by the U.S. National Science Teachers Association as the central goal for science instruction in a 1982 position statement. Several universities offered S/T/S courses and a national society was formed (Yager, 1996).

In practice, the U.S. version of S/T/S was based on assigning students a societal problem to solve or issue to address, or encouraging them to find one. After the problem is identified, students learn as much as they can about the problem. As they do this, students also learn some of the basic science related to the problem and the societal links. For instance, students might be concerned about the ecological impact of a local trash dump and investigate topics such as the water cycle, the biology and chemistry of decomposition. They may also learn about local politics and aspects of trash disposal and recycling.

By the end of the 20th century, enthusiasm for the S/T/S approach waned. Schools rarely provided the time necessary for S/T/S teaching and schools renewed concern that students learn basic science knowledge. Curriculum models were difficult to produce, there was little S/T/S instruction in teacher preparation programs, and inconclusive research results showing that S/T/S instruction was effective (Bennett, et al., 2007). Additionally, concerns lingered that targeting societal links must result in a lack of focus on core science concepts. (WM/KM)

Bennett, J., Lubben, F., & Hogarth, S. (2007). Bringing science to life: A synthesis of the research evidence on the effects of context-based and STS approaches to science teaching. *Science Education, 91*(3), 347-370.

DeBoer, G. E. (1991). *A history of ideas in science education: Implications for practice.* New York: Teachers College Press.

Gallagher, J. (1971). A broader base for science teaching. *Science Education, 55*(3), 329-338.

Yager, R. E. (1996). STS as a reform movement in science education. In R.E. Yager (Ed.), *Science/technology/society as reform in science education* (pp. 3-15). Albany, NY: State University of New York Press.

Ziman, J. (1980). *Teaching and learning about science and society.* Cambridge: Cambridge University Press.

Scientific Discourse (Rhetoric of Science) refers to the spoken and written means by which scientists discuss, share, persuade, and engage in argumentation (see also) to convince others of their ideas and conclusions (adapted from Atkinson, 1999; Horsella & Sindermann, 1992).

Two major implications for science education exist from the study of scientific discourse. First, students must understand the way in which scientists explain their work generally. Second, students should "do" science by producing arguments that approximate the current discussion among practicing scientists. Atkinson (1999) has shown that written scientific discourse uses specialized grammar, particular forms of narrative (such as passive voice), and format and elements contained in scientific reports (such as citing the work of others frequently), among other issues. Given the complexity of understanding scientific discourse, teachers must assist students explicitly rather than implicitly. For instance, students should have opportunities to hear scientists explain their discoveries and processes through media presentations or by reading written accounts of scientists' work as presented in publications. Students might also read scientists' actual accounts of discovery and realize how the nature of scientific discourse has changed through time.

A major element of scientific discourse is how the actual events of process and discovery in science are presented in the final journal article. For instance, much of the "messy" elements of science and the unproductive pathways are removed from when the final conclusions are written. Teachers must be skilled in helping students understand that the rhetoric of science may be somewhat different from the reality of science, an idea presented by Medawar (1963) in his classic paper.

Students should also be given opportunities to engage in the work of scientists in the most authentic way possible and present their findings (orally, as posters, or as papers). Science fairs (see also) and high level inquiry activities (see also) are particularly useful for this. Students fully engaged in science can engage in the discourse of science. If students are to act as scientists they must understand the discourse of science. Studies of scientific discourse acquisition show positive results (Rosebery et al., 1992; Herrenkohl & Guerra, 1998) as have related investigations designed to promote scientific argumentation (see also). (WM)

Atkinson, D. (1999). Language and science. *Annual Review of Applied Linguistics, 19*, 193-214.

Herrenkohl, L. R., & Guerra, M.R. (1998). Participant structures, scientific discourse, and student engagement in fourth grade. *Cognition and instruction, 16*(4), 431-473.

Horsella, M. & Sindermann, G. (1992). Aspects of scientific discourse: Argumentation. *English for Specific Purposes, 11*(2),129-139.

Medawar, P. B. (1963). Is the scientific paper a fraud? In P.B. Medawar (1990), *The threat and the glory: Reflections on science and scientists.* New York: Harper Collins.

Rosebery, A. S., Warren, B., & Conant, F. R. (1992). Appropriating scientific discourse: Findings from language minority classrooms. *Journal of the learning sciences, 2*(1), 61-92.

Scientific Literacy refers to the knowledge and understanding of scientific concepts and processes in order to make personal decisions, participate in civic and cultural affairs, and enter science and technology careers. What knowledge and skills a scientifically literate person should have is widely debated (Bybee, 1997). Shamos (1995) goes further and questions whether anyone can truly be scientifically literate given the criteria established by some.

A scientifically literate person can ask and find answers to everyday questions, can "describe, explain, and predict natural phenomena," can "read with understanding articles about science in the popular press and engage in social conversation," can "identify scientific issues underlying national and local decisions," can "express positions that are scientifically and technologically informed," can "evaluate the quality of scientific information on the basis of its source and the methods used to generate it," and can "pose and evaluate arguments based on evidence and apply conclusions from such arguments appropriately" (NRC, 1996, p. 22). Bybee (1997) suggests scientifically literate persons would have certain knowledge, values and sensibilities, along with problem-solving and critical thinking skills.

Scientific literacy is best seen as a continuum along which an individual progresses, not as an end state. This continuum has two dimensions – breadth and depth. Breadth ranges from recognition of vocabulary to conceptual understandings and then to a contextual understanding (Bybee, 1997). Depth involves an understanding of the scientific concepts, scientific inquiry, and the processes of science. Bybee's (1997) model of scientific literacy achieved throughout a lifetime includes the following:

- *Nominal literacy* – an understanding of basic concepts but with many inaccurate views and misconceptions about science.
- *Functional literacy* – the individual "… can read and write passages with simple scientific vocabulary" (pp. 84-85).
- *Conceptual and Procedural literacy* – "individuals demonstrate an understanding of both the parts and the whole of science and technology as disciplines…[and can] understand the structure of disciplines and the procedures for developing new knowledge and techniques" (p. 85).
- *Multidimensional literacy* – "consists of understanding the essential conceptual structures of science and technology as well as the features that make that understanding more complete … [these] individuals … understand the relationship of disciplines to the whole of science and technology and to society (p. 85)." (LW)

Bybee, R. W. (1997). *Achieving scientific literacy: From purposes to practices.* Portsmouth, NH: Heinemann.

National Research Council. (1996). *National science education standards.* Washington, DC: National Academy Press.

Shamos, M. (1995). *The myth of scientific literacy.* New Brunswick, NJ: Rutgers University Press.

Scientific Method (Scientific Methodology) describes all of the techniques, processes and logical routes used by scientists for exploring nature and investigating questions about the natural world. There is no single specific series of steps used by all scientists at all times (often called "*the*" scientific method).

For many years, philosophers of science including Feyeraband (1975), Bauer (1994) and Gjertsen (1989) have asked the question "is there a scientific method?" The answer is "yes" and "no." Yes, because there are things that most scientists do most of the time so these might be called scientific methods or methodology. No, because there is no formula or plan that all scientists follow all of the time as in the case of some single scientific method.

The key to understanding scientific methodology is to recognize that scientists use many techniques and logical processes to gain knowledge about the natural world. Scientists communicate with each other. Scientists generally review the literature to learn about past discoveries, take measurements and maintain careful records. Scientists apply creative thinking, develop and engage mathematical models, use the process of induction to evaluate data and look for patterns, and apply deduction to test their ideas. It would be impractical to list all of the things that scientists do as they explore and explain nature, but those things that scientists do routinely are very likely part of the methods of science.

Many science textbooks talk about *the* scientific method as if all scientists use the same process regularly. Often, this version of scientific method contains 6 to 9 steps beginning with "ask a question," continuing with "collect data" "analyze results" and ending with "communicate results." In many classrooms students are taught this step-by-step method directly and even assessed on their ability to memorize and report the steps.

Perhaps because scientists share their findings in scientific journals, using a standard reporting form, some may think that all scientists follow the same method to gain evidence and answer questions (Medawar, 1963). However, studies of scientists at work reveal many idiosyncratic [distinct and personal] ways of approaching research" and answering questions (McComas, 2004, p. 25).

If a student has no idea where to begin a scientific investigation, the step-by-step "scientific method" found in many science textbooks has value in providing a framework for such work but it should not be called *the* scientific method. There are many tools used by scientists to investigate nature and reach conclusions and such tools are the methods of science. (WM)

Bauer, H. H. (1994). *The myth of the scientific method.* Urbana: University of Illinois Press.

Feyerabend, P. (1975/2010). *Against method* (4th ed.). New York, NY: Verso Books.

Gjertsen, D. (1989). Is there a scientific method? In *Science and philosophy: Past and present.* New York: Penguin Books.

McComas, W. F. (2004). Keys to teaching the nature of science: Focusing on the nature of science in the science classroom. *The Science Teacher, 71*(9), 24-27.

Medawar, P. B. (1963). Is the scientific paper a fraud? In P. B. Medawar (1963/1990), *The threat and the glory* (pp. 228-233). New York: Harper Collins.

Scientific Model (Modeling) is a simulation that might result in an actual tangible product or structure or a virtual one (such as a prediction or other product generated and visualized using a computer) that " abstracts and simplifies a system by focusing on key features to explain and predict scientific phenomena" (Schwarz et al., 2009, p. 633). Models are useful in teaching because they provide a more concrete representation of some phenomenon but may also be helpful when the real laboratory activity is expensive, time consuming, or dangerous, and/or assist students in collecting data and making predictions.

According to Johnson and Lesh (2003, p. 274), a model must consist of "elements, relations, operations, and rules governing interactions …'' For instance, scientists interested in studying water flow in a river might produce a scaled-down version of the river in the laboratory based on the length and width of the river including the same kind of rock found in the river. Then the scientists might run water through the model to determine what happens. Another approach is to use a computer to simulate the set of known variables and then run virtual experiments to see the outcome. The most useful models most accurately simulate the actual phenomenon. For instance, a volcano model made with food coloring, baking soda, and vinegar does not simulate actual lava flowing from a volcano and might ultimately result in the formation of misconceptions.

Modeling relatively simple phenomena (such as the flow of a river) might best be accomplished using a physical representation, but modeling very complex systems with many variables (such as climate change) can only be accomplished using powerful computers and sophisticated programming. Common models in science include the food web, the Bohr model of the atom, and the use of light rays to demonstrate vision (Schwarz, 2009).

In science models are useful for running multiple trials and for making predictions. This is also true in science instruction, but models can also support student understanding of the core concepts of science (Lehrer and Schauble, 2006). Models also provide opportunities for students to experience a phenomenon in a hands-on (see also) setting. Only if students really understand a scientific phenomenon could they accurately model it, therefore model making can be used as an assessment tool. (AR)

Johnson, T., & Lesh, R. (2003). Technology-based represetnational media. In R. Lesh & H. M. Doerr (Eds.), *Beyond constructivism: Models and modeling perspectives on mathematics problem solving, learning, and teaching* (pp. 265-278). Mahwah, NJ: Erlbaum.

Lehrer, R., & Schauble, L. (2006). Scientific thinking and science literacy: Supporting development in learning in contexts. In W. Damon, R. M. Lerner, K. A. Renninger, & I. E. Sigel (Eds.), *Handbook of child psychology* (6th ed., Vol. 4). Hoboken, NJ: John Wiley and Sons.

Schwarz, C., Reiser, B. J., Davis, E. A., Kenyon, L. O., Archer, A., Fortus, D., et al. (2009). Developing a learning progression for scientific modeling: Making scientific modeling accessible and meaningful for learners. *Journal of Research in Science Teaching, 46*(6), 632-654.

Scientific Openness refers to the degree of sharing of data and conclusions by scientists as they conduct investigations and report results. There is a growing trend to make raw data available to others as quickly as possible and to provide reports and articles even before they are available in printed journals

Openness and Data. A long-standing norm of science is that all data should be available for review by others. Recently, many scientists and scientific societies (Royal Society, 2012) have advocated that even as data are generated, these data should be shared with the wider scientific community. This idea is called "open notebook" or "open data" science. An advantage to this level of openness is that other experts in the field may be informed by results as they are gathered without having to wait for final publication (which rarely includes raw data anyway). Occasionally work reported through the "open notebook" plan has been shown to be incorrect when outside experts reviewed it real time. Wald (2010) points out that when these outside experts report back to those who gathered the data, errors can be quickly corrected. Unfortunately, there are other cases where potential rivals have become collaborators because they have discovered shared interests.

Of course not everyone agrees with this degree of openness. Scientists working in industrial settings where profit is the goal are particularly concerned that sharing data could potentially invite others to steal important information that might have resulted in products and patents for the company that initially invested in the research. Other scientists are concerned about the issue of priority and are worried that releasing data too early might enable others to solve problems first and make important discoveries. Finally, some scientists are concerned that criminals and terrorists might make use of the data if such information were readily available.

Openness and Publication. Many scientists support the idea of publishing conclusions as quickly as possible to inform scientific work being conducted elsewhere and for use in practical applications, such as medicine, without delay. This idea is called "open source" or "open access" publication. In many instances, the work of scientists is supported by governments and private foundations leading to the question of "who owns science?" If the work has been paid for by the public, many scientists believe that it should be available to the public as quickly as possible. Publishers primarily are concerned that if articles are available on the Web their business may be negatively impacted. Some scientists are worried that direct publishing may damage the quality control promoted by peer review and the prestige associated with publishing in the most important journals.

It is possible to simulate and discuss these principles of "openness" in the science classroom by having students work together on investigations and share data as has been recommended through the "open notebook" (see science notebook). (WM)

Royal Society. (2012, June). *Science as an open enterprise.* London: The Royal Society Science Policy Centre.
Wald, C. (2010, April 9). Scientists embrace openness. 10.1126/science.caredit.a1000036

Scientific Thinking Skills are those traits, characteristics and thinking methods employed by scientists to explore and address problems in the natural world.

Although there is no definitive list of scientific thinking skills, many authorities would agree that such skills include "reasoning and thinking skills involved in students' scientific inquiry, such as hypothesis generation, experimental design, evidence evaluation and drawing inferences" (Zimmerman, 2007, p. 174). In addition to the skills previously mentioned, some equate scientific thinking with science processes (see also), which include observing, using space/time relationships, using numbers, inferring, measuring, communicating, classifying and predicting, controlling variables, defining operationally, formulating hypotheses, interpreting data, and experimenting (American Association for the Advancement of Science, 1967).

However, more sophisticated studies consider only the "integrated" processes that might lead directly to the consideration and solution of problems using a "scientific" approach (Kuhn et al., 1988; Kuhn, 1993). In an extensive review of the literature, Zimmerman (2007) concludes that *scientific thinking* is best defined as the "application of methods or principles of scientific inquiry to reasoning or problem-solving situations, and involves the skills implicated in generating, testing and revising theories, and in the case of fully developed skills, to reflect on the process of knowledge acquisition and change" (p.173).

Education researchers such as Williams et al. (2003) have long been interested in the ways that students engage in scientific thinking including the evaluation of evidence, what happens when students encounter surprising data, the relationship of cause and effect, the elements of experimental design and interpretation including the nature of observations, hypothesis formation, the isolation and control of variables, and "thinking with data." Clearly, with these studies as a guide, the best definition for scientific thinking skills extends well beyond the basic science process skills and inhabits the more sophisticated realm inhabited by science learners as they consider problems while thinking *as* scientists. (WM)

American Association for the Advancement of Science. (1967). *Science – A process approach.* Washington, DC: Author.

Kuhn, D. (1993). Science as argument: Implications for teaching and learning scientific thinking. *Science Education, 77*(3), 319-337.

Kuhn, D., Amsel, E., & O'Loughlin, M. (1988). *The development of scientific thinking skills.* Orlando, FL: Academic Press.

Williams, W. M., Papierno, P. B., Makel, M. C., & Ceci, S. J. (2003). Thinking like a scientist about real-world problems: The Cornell institute for research on children science education program. *Journal of Applied Developmental Psychology, 25*(1), 107-126.

Zimmerman, C. (2007). The development of scientific thinking skills in elementary and middle school. *Developmental Review, 27*(2), 172-223.

Scientific Writing Heuristic (SWH) is a structured teaching plan (i.e., a heuristic) designed to help learners gain understanding while engaged in laboratory activities. In SWH, instructors use effective teaching strategies (such as asking effective questions, using wait-time, responding appropriately and using students' ideas) and have students write about and produce diagrams of their ideas (claims) by comparing them to the actual evidence gained from the laboratory activity.

SWH was developed by Keys, Hand, Prain and Collins (Keys et al., 1999) and has two essential sets of guidelines, one for the teacher and another to assist students as they collect data in the laboratory. Since writing and the production of diagrams to link evidence and claims is such an important part of the strategy for the students, SWH is often called "writing to learn science" (Hand et al., 2004, p. 131).

Burke et al. (2006) discuss the use of this strategy in the chemistry laboratory and describe SWH as "an instructional technique that combines inquiry tasks, collaborative work, and writing, while providing a structure for both students and instructors to do effective activities in the ... laboratory" (p. 1032). They provide a useful outline of how the plan is used with pre-laboratory discussion, asking initial questions, collecting data, making claims based on evidence, and reflecting on these claims. SWH also uses a laboratory report format that reinforces these elements. Burke et al. (2006) notes the teacher's role in the SWH that includes facilitating student progress "without dictating procedures and approaches or directly answering questions" (p. 1036). Instructors should be encouraging, act as coaches and not leaders, and assist students in finding meaning in the data and observations from the laboratory activity. Of course, these are all previously well-established research-based teacher behaviors that are not unique to the SWH approach.

Studies investigating the effectiveness of this approach generally show good results. For instance, Akkus et al. (2007) show that SWH positively impacts students' post-test achievement when compared with more traditional methods of instruction although how much of the impact is due to the previously established teacher behaviors or to the SWH has not yet been established. (WM)

Akkus, R, Gunnel, M., & Hand, B. (2007). Comparing an inquiry-based approach known as the science writing heuristic to traditional science teaching practices: Are there differences? *International Journal of Science Education, 29*(14), 1745-1765.

Burke, K. A., Greenbowe, T. J., & Hand, B. M. (2006). Implementing the science writing heuristic in the chemistry laboratory. *Journal of chemical education, 83*(7), 1032-1038.

Keys, C. W., Hand, B., Prain, V., & Collins, S. (1999). Using the science writing heuristic as a tool for learning from laboratory investigations in secondary science. *Journal of Research in Science Teaching, 36*(10), 1065-1084.

Hand, B., Wallace, C. W., & Yang, Eun-Mi. (2004). Using a science writing heuristic to enhance learning outcomes from laboratory activities in seventh grade science: Quantitative and qualitative aspects. *International Journal of Science Education, 26*(2), 131-149.

Situated Learning occurs when a learner is immersed and heavily involved in an experience that may provide opportunities for them to gain new knowledge and/or skills. This form of learning combines understanding from past experience and current observations in the field.

Situated learning places a student in a setting that is often outside of the classroom such as a science center, zoo, museum, laboratory or natural area (see outdoor education and informal science learning). By doing this, the process of gaining knowledge is contextualized in an experiential framework (Lave & Wenger, 1991). Situated learning is facilitated by applying concepts and past experiences to current observations. Knowledge transfer is supported as students test their former learning in conjunction with interpreting new findings in the situated learning space (Putnam & Borko, 2000). The situated learning approach contrasts with the standard model of teaching where students gain new knowledge prescribed by teachers and textbooks. A significant benefit of situated learning is that it is a different approach from traditional instruction. The well-known philosopher of education, John Dewey, was one of the primary proponents for integrating experience into education and saw it as tantamount to providing a complete education to students (Dewey, 1916). This integration prepares the students for their future in life, not just the classroom.

Active involvement in society and pursuing a career require a degree of situational learning. Themes of this space include collaboration and discussion between participants. It is these interactions with people and the surrounding environment that provide inputs to understanding. The social nature of situated learning encourages the student to discuss their conceptions and knowledge with others. Students become partners in the learning space rather than just receivers of knowledge from teachers. Situated learning provides students with new learning opportunities and instances to apply their knowledge to real-world situations.

Field trips are common examples of situated learning in science education. A trip to a science center or an excursion to the outdoors can supply many situated learning opportunities. In either setting, students are immersed in experiences that meet the criteria for new observations in the field. Students are easily excited by field trips and a well-planned situated learning experience can vastly improve the learning in the classroom by providing contextualization for course discussions. (JK)

Dewey, J. (1916). *Democracy and education: An introduction to the philosophy of education*. New York: Macmillan.

Lave, J., & Wenger, E. (1991). *Situated learning: Legitimate peripheral participation*. Cambridge, UK: University of Cambridge Press.

Putnam, R., & Borko, H. (2000). What do new views of knowledge and thinking have to say about research on teacher learning? *Educational Researcher, 29*(1), 4-15.

Social Constructivism refers to the notion that people form, or construct knowledge as they interact with others to share, compare, and debate as learners (Applefield et al., 2001). This social construction also includes modeling behaviors observed in the interaction with others.

Social constructivism posits that learning occurs within groups of individuals. Those who participate in the activities and work of the group build knowledge in the process (Woolfolk, 2011). Learning occurs as learners refine their own understandings and help others do the same (Applefield, et al., 2001). In social constructivist classrooms, collaborative and social interactions among students and between students and the teacher are prominent.

Lev Vygotsky, the father of social constructivism (Powell & Kalina, 2010), studied how language development influences higher cognitive functions (Hodson & Hodson, 1998). According to Vygotsky, "Language enhances learning and precedes knowledge or thinking" (Powell & Kalina, 2010, p. 248). Cooperative learning (used during inquiry activities, conducting research, and project development) and scaffolding, and assisting students until they can progress on their own, are important attributes of social constructivism. Vygotsky asserted that what children can do with the assistance of more capable others is more indicative of their mental development than what they can do on their own (Gordon, 2009).

Paulo Freire contributed to social constructivism with his view that learning is based on dialogue; students are both learners and teachers as their roles change frequently in the process of learning (Gordon, 2009). Students become co-teachers; teachers become students and learn through dialogue with their students. He asserted that knowledge is acquired through inquiry *and* meaning making (see also) as is the case with all constructivist learning theories.

The role of language (a type of social construct) is a key element in social constructivism since it is vital in receiving information and organizing meaning (Hodson & Hodson, 1998). Like cognitive constructivism, social constructivism occurs only with respect for what students already know, think, and understand (Patchen & Cox-Peterson, 2008). (PW)

Applefield, J. M., Huber, M., & Moallem, M. (2001). Constructivism in theory and practice: Toward a better understanding. *The High School Journal, 84*(2), 35-53.

Gordon, M. (2009). Toward a pragmatic discourse of constructivism: Reflections on lessons from practice. *Educational Studies, 45*(1), 39-58.

Hodson, D., & Hodson, J. (1998). From constructivism to social constructivism: A Vygotskian perspective on teaching and learning science. *School Science Review, 79*(289), 33-41.

Patchen, T., & Cox-Peterson, A. (2008).Constructing cultural relevance in science: A case study of two elementary teachers. *Science Education, 92*(6), 994-1014.

Powell, K. C., & Kalina, C. (2010). Cognitive and social constructivism: Developing tools for an effective classroom. *Education, 130*(2), 241-250.

Woolfolk, A. (2011). *Educational psychology* (11th ed.). Boston, MA: Pearson.

Socio-scientific Issue-based Instruction is an extension of the Science, Technology, and Society and Problem-based approaches to science teaching (see also) in which science content is placed in a social context (see contextual and situated science learning) to provide students with an authentic view of how the science relates to the real world (Zeidler et al., 2005).

Typically, science content is taught with few references to the impact that the content may have on society. Science, Technology, and Society was designed to change this situation by embedding instruction in a situation that puts science content in a practical frame. Socio-scientific issue-based instruction (SSI) adds to this plan by "requiring a degree of moral reasoning or the evaluation of ethical concerns in the process of arriving at decisions regarding possible resolution of those issues. The intent is that such issues are personally meaningful and engaging to students, require the use of evidence-based reasoning, and provides a context for understanding scientific information" (Zeidler & Nicols, 2009, p. 49).

Zeidler and Nicols add that the issues are usually controversial and "involve the deliberate use of scientific topics that require students to engage in dialogue, discussion and debate" (p. 49). Others (Sadler et al., 2007) agree, stating that socio-scientific issues are controversial, socially relevant, real-world problems informed by science, and often include an ethical component. This component and the resulting debate involving students provide the central characteristics of SSI.

A number of areas have been proposed as sources of potential socio-scientific issues including debates about nuclear power, global warming, genetic testing, stem cell research, end of life issues, transplantation, bio-fuels, etc. Klosterman and Sadler (2010) remind us that students cannot solve the issue of global warming, for example, but will develop a position based upon the information they discover by exploring the issue and learning related science content.

Ratcliffe and Grace (2003) suggest that the most appropriate issues to support an SSI approach have a basis in cutting edge science, involve making choices and forming opinions, are media-supported, deal with incomplete or conflicting information, address local, national or global dimensions, involve cost-benefit considerations, and require consideration of values and ethical reasoning. (WM)

Klosterman, M. L., & Sadler, T. D. (2010). Multi-level assessment of scientific content knowledge gains associated with socioscientific issues-based instruction. *International Journal of Science Education. 32*(8), 1017-1043.

Ratcliffe, M., & Grace, M. (2003). *Science education for citizenship: Teaching socio-scientific issues.* Philadelphia: Open University Press.

Sadler, T. D., Barab, S. A., & Scott, B. (2007). What do students gain by engaging in socio-scientific inquiry? *Research in Science Education, 37*(4), 371-391.

Zeidler, D. L. & Nicols, B.H (2009). Socioscientific issues: Theory and practice. *Journal of Elementary Science Education, 21*(2), 49-58.

Zeidler, D. L., Sadler, T. D., Simmons, M. L., & Howes, E. V. (2005). Beyond STS: A research-based framework for socioscientific issues education. *Science Education, 89*(3), 357-377.

Standards (Academic Standards) in Science Teaching are statements suggesting or even mandating what students should know, understand, and be able to do at a particular grade/age level in a given school subject.

The development of such standards has given rise to what is often called standards-based education, a plan by which there are clear, measureable objectives for all students. In standards based education, how much students achieve in school is compared to these concrete standards or goals, not to other students (Parkay et al., 2010).

Standards documents are typically prepared by local school districts, professional associations, and other educational agencies. There are usually two types of standards: content and performance (Parkay et al., 2010). Science content standards refer to the content students should know, understand and apply (National Research Council [NRC], 1996). If some level of understanding is prescribed, then the term performance standard is often used to link to some level of proficiency (Parkay et al., 2010).

Science content standards are commonly referred to as the "what" of science content. Standards, however, are not considered a curriculum (see also). Rather, standards should inform the development of the curriculum, which is the actual plan for instruction. Educational leaders and others interested in teaching and learning can use the standards as a guide to develop curriculum and assessments of student learning. Teachers use standards to develop more specific objectives for units of study and instructional activities as well as for classroom assessments and even larger evaluations of the effectiveness of schooling when comparing one region to another or one nation to others. Parents and the community members can use the standards to assess the quality of education in their local school districts (Parkay et al., 2010). Ideally, once standards are developed they will be used to guide the content of teacher preparation programs, classroom teaching, professional development plans, student assessments, and textbooks.

At the U.S. national level, science standards documents include the *National Science Education Standards* (NSES) (see also) and the *Benchmarks for Science Literacy (see also)*. Periodically, education leaders call for improvements in the existing K-12 science education standards to reflect recent advances in science, to include the newest research about how students learn science, and to ensure that new graduates have the knowledge and skills to succeed in college and in a highly competitive global society. Therefore, a new document containing objectives for science teaching, called the *Next Generation Science Standards* (see also), has just been released. It remains to be seen how many of the U.S. states will adopt these recommendations in some form. (PW)

National Research Council. (1996). *National science education standards.* Washington, DC: National Academy Press.

Parkay, F., Antcil, E. J., & Haas, G. (2010). *Curriculum leadership: Readings for developing quality educational programs* (9th ed.). Boston, MA: Allyn & Bacon.

STEM: Science, Technology, Engineering, and Mathematics is an acronym commonly used to refer to one or more of the four disciplines (science, technology, engineering, and/or mathematics) that are seen as related to each other. These are seen as vital elements in preparing the next generation of technological and scientifically literate citizens and those employed in integrated fields such as medicine, computer science, agriculture, and others.

According to Sanders (2009), the National Science Foundation (NSF) in the 1990's began to use the acronym SMET, as a "… shorthand, for 'science, mathematics, engineering, and technology'" (p. 20). SMET was perceived to sound too much like "smut" and STEM, became the acronym of choice. While this may explain the modern label, "interest in education involving the study of the STEM subjects began in the colonial era …" (Salinger & Zuga, 2009, p. 4). They further note that the U.S. federal government has offered continual support for career and technology education though legislation such as the *Vocational Education Act of 1917*. Bybee (2010) notes that even before the term STEM was coined, the "The STEM community responded vigorously to produce the Sputnik-spurred education reforms of the 1960s" (p. 996).

The 1983 U.S. *Nation at Risk* report suggested that the nation was headed toward an "Economic Sputnik" (Marcuccio, 1987) in part because of the decline in preparation for careers in science and technology. This in turn, spurred the National Science Foundation to expand funding to include engineering education (Salinger & Zuga, 2009). The S/T/S movement (see also) shed additional light on the urgency to prepare students more effectively in the disciplines now known as STEM by ensuring that students engage with larger societal issues, understand the science *and technology* within that context and their impact within that context, and not just learn the content itself (Deboer, 2000).

Many suggest that instead of thinking of STEM as four separate elements that are more or less related, STEM might be considered as a single overarching concept from which individuals draw when generating or validating new knowledge, solutions to problems or in the production of products. Therefore, STEM may be thought of as a reference to the fields in which scientists, engineers, and mathematicians work. STEM *education* therefore "includes approaches that explore teaching and learning between/among any two or more of the STEM subject areas, and/or between a STEM subject and one or more other school subjects" (Sanders, 2009, p. 21).

Roberts (2012) has observed that even though STEM has been growing as an initiative for more than 20 years, schools are now trying to understand how it should be used in instruction. Although the term STEM still has many different meanings in different educational contexts, most agree that the four allied areas have more in common with each other than with other school subjects and, for that reason, should be considered together for instructional purposes. As the field matures and the term STEM is used more frequently, is vital to ensure that those discussing STEM clarify their definition. Many now routinely define STEM as "integrated" while others maintain a family resemblance model whereby the four elements of STEM maintain some discreteness.

The goal of STEM literacy seems to recommend an interdisciplinary instructional approach (see blended science) which couples the study of rigorous academic concepts in real-world contexts so that students connect science, technology, engineering, and mathematics with school, community, work, and global issues while developing skills necessary to compete in the new economy (Tsupros et al., 2009).

Application of STEM in school settings might utilize Purposeful Design and Inquiry (PD&I), a teaching approach that combines scientific inquiry with technological design. "Following the PD&I approach, students envisioning and developing solutions to a design challenge might, for example wish to test their ideas about various materials and designs, or the impact of external factors (e.g., air, water, temperature, friction, etc.) upon those materials and designs" (Sanders, 2009, p. 21). This is also a form of Problem Based Learning (see also) combining mathematics and scientific inquiry within the context of a technological design problem. Prior to the integration of STEM in education, scientific-based inquiry (see also) rarely occurred in a technology setting, and technology design problems were rarely seen in the science laboratory (Sanders, 2009).

The U.S. *Next Generation Science Standards* (see also) have embraced some elements of the integrated STEM instructional approach discussed here. Time will tell if these new standards can remove the silos and other barriers that the science, technology, engineering and math communities have defended as their "sovereign territories" (Sanders, 2009, p. 21).

While the current focus of a STEM instructional orientation will likely have positive outcomes, educators should be cautious about "STEMmania" (Sanders, 2009) and ensure that students are always able to distinguish the unique and individual elements that define each of the four STEM disciplines. Problems in science will always be distinct from those in engineering just as motivations in science will be different from those in technology. There are also important practical and fiscal considerations with respect to teacher preparation at both the preservice and inservice levels. (JH/WM)

Bybee, R. (2010). What is stem education? *Science, 329*, 996.

DeBoer, G. E. (2000). Scientific literacy: Another look at its historical and contemporary meanings and its relationship to science education reform. *Journal of Research in Science Teaching, 37*(6), 582-601.

Marcuccio, P. R. (1987). Forty-five years of elementary school science: A guided tour. *Science and Children, 24*(4), 12-15.

Roberts, A. (2012). A justification for STEM education. *Technology and Engineering Teacher*. http://www.iteaconnect.org/mbrsonly/Library/TTT/TTTe/04-12roberts.pdf.

Salinger, G., & Zuga, K. (2009). Background and history of the STEM movement. *The Overlooked STEM Imperatives: Technology and Engineering*. iteaconnect.org.

Sanders, M. (2009, December). STEM, STEM education, STEMmania. *The Technology Teacher, 68*(4), 20-26.

Tsupros, N., Kohler, R., & Hallinen, J. (2009). *STEM education: A project to identify the missing components*. Intermediate Unit 1: Center for STEM Education and Leonard Gelfand Center for Service Learning and Outreach, Carnegie Mellon University, Pennsylvania.

Summative Assessments are student evaluations (tests or other measures) that occur often (but not always) at the end of a course, module, or unit to measure how well the students have met the goals of instruction. The "final exam," is a traditional kind of summative assessment. Summative exams contrast with formative assessments (see also) that occur *during* instruction.

According to Harlen and James (1997), summative assessments have a number of characteristics including thra they:

- take place at certain intervals when achievement has to be reported,
- relate to a learning progression (see also) when measured against some criteria like standards (see also) or benchmarks (see also),
- allow student results to be compared against each other because they are based on the same criteria,
- involve some quality assurance procedures, and
- should be based on evidence from the full range of performance relevant to the criteria being used.

Summative assessments are always compared to formative assessments because both relate to assessing the learning process. The main difference between summative and formative assessments is that summative assessments are considered assessment *of* learning, while formative assessments are considered assessment *for* learning.

Harlen and Deakin-Crick (2002) indicate several advantages for the use of summative assessment. To indicate whether the goals (or standards) of instruction have been met and enable schools to monitor progress toward these goals. Summative assessments raise expectations, and they cause teachers, schools, and students to place more effort into the standards due to rewards and penalties associated with the results of these tests.

Negative impacts from summative assessments can be minimized by ensuring that standards are worth achieving, ensuring summative assessment that target the standards are valid and reliable, avoiding drill and practice for tests, de-emphasizing one type of test and using a variety of assessment types, recognizing the limitations of tests, preventing the content and methods of teaching from being limited by the form and content of tests, and avoiding children being faced with tests in which they are unlikely to succeed.

As an example, a summative assessment could permit a biology teacher to measure student understanding at the end of a unit on plant structure and function and take that into account before designing the next lessons on plant growth and development. (AR)

Harlen, W., & Deakin-Crick, R. (2002). *A systematic review of the impact of summative assessment and tests on students' motivation for learning.* London, UK: Evidence for Policy and Practice Information and Coordinating Centre.
Harlen, W., & James, M. (1997). Assessment and learning: Differences and relationships between formative and summative assessment. *Assessment in Education, 4*(3), 365-379.

Teaching for Conceptual Understanding is a purpose for teaching and learning through which students develop deep knowledge of a concept and can use, predict, explain and argue based on this knowledge. Understanding in this context is more than memorization, identification, or the ability to put values into a formula and solve problems in a rote fashion.

The terms "knowledge" and "understanding" are often thought of as synonyms, but there is an important distinction. *To know* means that one may recall facts and information accurately, but understanding connotes the ability to use information in a flexible fashion in multiple environments and circumstances (McDiarmid et al., 1989).

Students usually do not gain understanding as a result of traditional teaching where information is merely shared with students somewhat passively (see didactic instruction). True understanding is achieved when students are given time to process and reflect on an idea, particularly when caused to challenge present conceptions. Making generalizations and connections to other phenomena, discovering new insights, making sense out of prior experiences, and developing big picture concepts are indicators of understanding. Students who really understand can draw useful inferences, make connections among facts, explain their conclusions in their *own* words, and apply their learning by transferring it to new situations with appropriate flexibility and fluency (Wiggins & McTighe, 2011).

With this definition of "understanding" in mind, it will be clear that teaching for conceptual understanding is more complex than teaching to support recall. In a constructivist fashion (see also) instructors must directly confront students' prior knowledge (Posner et al., 1982). In doing so students will solidify what they already know and transform it into true understanding if that prior knowledge is consonant with the current scientific worldview. In contrast, if students' prior knowledge is scientifically inaccurate, teachers can challenge such perceptions by giving students opportunities to explore concepts more deeply and arrive at true understanding. In such cases, teaching for understanding becomes teaching for conceptual change.

Nothing can guarantee that students fully "understand" a concept, but considering students' prior conceptions while providing opportunities to apply what has been learned are strongly recommended when teaching for conceptual understanding. (PW)

McDiarmid W., Ball, D. L., & Anderson, C. (1989). Why staying ahead one chapter just won't work: Subject-specific pedagogy. In M. C. Reynolds (Ed.), *Knowledge base for the beginning teacher* (pp. 193-205). New York: Pergamon Press.

Posner, G. J., Strike, K. A., Hewson, P. W., & Gertzog, W. A. (1982). Accommodation of a scientific conception: Towards a theory of conceptual change. *Science Education, 66*(2), 211-227.

Wiggins, G., & McTighe, J. (2011). *The understanding by design guide to creating high-quality units.* Alexandria, VA: ASCD.

Technological Pedagogical Content Knowledge (TPACK) is a proposed set of competencies consisting of the intersection of three constructs; pedagogical knowledge (PK), content knowledge (CK), and knowledge of technology in the service of education (TK). This new domain (TPACK) assists educational professionals in recognizing that the classroom use of technology must be informed by an understanding of other forms of knowledge that guide classroom practice.

TPACK is expanded from Shulman's (1986) work in defined types of teacher knowledge and was first introduced by Mishra and Kohler in 2006. TPACK is the space formed where two of Shulman's "teacher knowledge" circles overlap. The new domain, technology, intersects with knowledge of content and pedagogy to include another skill set by which teachers need to reach students most effectively. It is not a construct of isolated knowledge bases, but emphasizes new kinds of knowledge that may become apparent at the intersection.

If one considers P and C together you get Shulman's PCK. Similarly, T and C taken together, you get Technological Content Knowledge (TCK), knowledge of the relationship between technology and content. At the intersection of T and P, is Technological Pedagogical Knowledge (TPK), which emphasizes how various technologies are used in the settings for teaching and learning.

The TPACK framework makes it clear that just helping teachers use available instructional technologies is not sufficient for effective implementation. Teachers must be given opportunities to develop appropriate, context-specific strategies for integrating technology into their teaching as is the case with knowledge of content and pedagogical tools. TPACK informs teachers how technology integration is a negotiation between the relationships between the other competencies of P and C so that infusing technology into best teaching practices does not isolate the technology but seamlessly assimilates into those best practices. (LA)

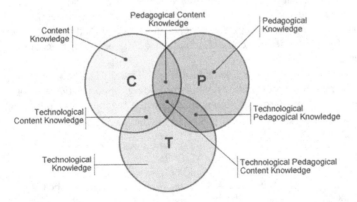

From Mishra and Koehler (2006) and found at www.tpak.org

Mishra, P., & Koehler, M. J. (2006). Technological pedagogical content knowledge: A new framework for teacher knowledge. *Teachers College Record, 108*(6), 1017-1054.
Shulman, L. S. (1986). Those who understand: Knowledge growth in teaching. *Educational Researcher, 15*(2), 4-14.

Theory in Science is typically a complex expression often involving unobservable entities (Campbell, 1953) is a statement explaining how a law may function in the way that it does. A scientific theory is "a well substantiated explanation of some aspect of the natural world that can incorporate facts, laws, inferences, and tested hypotheses" (National Academy of Sciences, 1998, p. 5).

As an example, consider "molecular theory." This theory explains the various individual gas laws. Molecular theory states that all matter is made of tiny particles and these particles bump into each other more frequently when the temperature increases. We know that the volume of a gas increases when the temperature increases. This relationship of temperature and volume is called a law. Molecular "theory" was proposed to tell us why the various gas laws operate in the way that the do (McComas, 2004).

Scientific theories:

A) may be validated by hypothetico-deductive testing;
B) are supported by and based on many facts, scientific investigations, observations and even laws;
C) are broad, comprehensive and unifying statements (sometimes making use of insights from different disciplines);
D) explain *natural phenomena* such as events, observations, relationships (in other words, they explain laws of nature);
E) are generally considered to have been invented rather than discovered.

There are countless theories found in all of the sciences including the *Theory of Plate Tectonics* in physics and earth science which explain continental drift, the *Kinetic Molecular Theory of Matter* in chemistry which explains Boyle's Law, and the *Germ Theory* in biology which explains the cause of illness and related phenomena.

Many science teachers and textbooks wrongly suggest that laws are more important than theories. Some even state that theories will become laws with increasing evidence to support them. These statements are both untrue. Laws and theories are both very important kinds of scientific information but they explain different types of phenomena (McComas, 2003). Theories do not become laws although law-like relationships may be found in the complete structure of theories. (WM)

Campbell, N. (1953). *What is science?* New York: Dover.
McComas, W. F. (2003). A textbook case: Laws and theories in biology instruction. *International Journal of Science and Mathematics Education, 1*(2), 1-15.
McComas, W. F. (2004). Keys to teaching the nature of science: Focusing on the nature of science in the science classroom. *The Science Teacher, 71*(9), 24-27.
National Academy of Sciences (NAS). (1998). *Teaching about evolution and the nature of science.* Washington, DC: National Academy Press.

Trends in International Mathematics and Science Study (**TIMSS**) is an international assessment measuring science and mathematics achievement of 4th and 8th grade students that can be compared to students in other countries. TIMSS has many of the same goals as does PISA (see also).

The TIMSS assessments began in 1995 and have been administered every four years with the next administration scheduled for 2015. In 2011, over 60 countries and other educational systems participated. TIMSS also administers a TIMSS Assessments that measures trends in advanced mathematics and physics among students during their last year of secondary school. The advance assessment was conducted in 1995 and 2008 and will be administered again in 2015.

Countries participate in and use TIMSS results "to explore educational issues, including: monitoring system-level achievement trends in global context, establishing achievement goals and standards for educational improvement, simulating curriculum reform, improving teaching and learning through research and analysis of data, conducting related studies ..., and training researchers and teachers in assessment and evaluation" (TIMSS & PIRLS International Study Center, 2011, p. 1).

In 2011, 550,000 students from around the world participated on the TIMSS assessment including 20,000 students from across 1000 schools from the United States. The data from the various administrations of TIMSS are widely available with country-by-country comparisons discussed frequently in both the popular and education press. One very good source of information regarding TIMMS from the U.S. perspective may be found at http://nces.ed.gov/Timss/. (CB)

National Center for Education Statistics. (2013). Trends in international mathematics and science study (TIMSS). Institute of Education Sciences. Retrieved from http://nces.ed.gov/Timss/

TIMSS, & PIRLS International Study Center (2011). *About TIMSS and PIRLS*. Chestnut Hill, MA: Author. Retrieved from http://timssandpirls.bc.edu/home/pdf/TP_About.pdf

Urban Science Education relates to the teaching of science with respect to the unique opportunities and challenges found in urban areas.

Although criteria defining "what is urban" differ (Paddison, 2001), about half the human population (and nearly 80% of the U.S. population) resides in metropolitan areas compared to 10% at the beginning of the last century. Urban areas are typically distinguished from non-urban areas based on: high population density, diverse economic activity that is largely non-agricultural, and increased home to work commuting patterns.

Barton and Tobin (2001) remind us that urban areas often support wide diversity that often includes large immigrant populations. Urban centers may lack open space and are overcrowded; have higher crime levels and more pollution. Many, but not all, urban areas include changing student demographics, high levels of poverty, and students who are not proficient in math and literacy along with higher teacher turnover (attrition) not typically seen in suburban areas.

Many science education researchers have "been working in urban settings attempting to understand what it means to create inclusive and empowering science teaching and learning settings for urban students in poverty" (Barton & Tobin, 2011, p. 844). Researchers recommend that the following issues and strategies should be considered to enhance urban teaching. Others would argue that these notions represent good teaching generally, not just urban teaching:

1. Consider how capitalism drives education and science practices to support a more equitable and socially just society (Barton, 2001ab).
2. Focus science instruction on "how" science is learned and not just on the content of science. The culture of science should empower urban learners and provide meaningful connections to their needs, ideas, beliefs, and particular community (Fusco, 2001).
3. Have urban students tackle real-world science problems through school-community partnerships, blending community-based with school-based knowledge (Bouillon & Gomez, 2001).
4. Pair novice teachers with master teachers so new teachers can see first-hand how to handle challenging situations (Tobin et al., 2001). (CB)

Barton, A. C. (2001a). Capitalism, critical pedagogy, and urban science education: Interview with Peter McLaren. *Journal of Research in Science Teaching, 38*(8), 847-859.
Barton, A. C. (2001b). Science education in urban settings: Seeking new ways of praxis through ethnography. *Journal of Research in Science Teaching, 38*(8), 899-917.
Barton, A. C., & Tobin, K. (2001). Urban science education. *Journal of Research in Science Teaching, 38*(8), 843-846.
Bouillon, L. M., & Gomez, L. M. (2001). Connecting school and community with science learning. Real world problems and school-community partnerships as contextual scaffolds. *Journal of Research in Science Teaching, 38*(8), 878-898.
Fusco, D. (2001). Creating relevant science through urban planning and gardening. *Journal of Research in Science Teaching, 38*(8), 860-877.
Paddison, R. (2001). *Handbook of urban studies.* London, UK: Sage.
Tobin, K., Roth, W. M., & Zimmerman, A. (2001). Learning to teach science in urban schools. *Journal of Research in Science Teaching, 38*(8), 941-964.

Virtual Learning Environment (VLE) is an integrated multimedia teaching environment designed in principle so that students can do everything that occurs in traditional schools, but do so through the internet (Kumar et al., 1998).

According to Kumar (1998) VLE is a self-contained web based system that requires no other technology to offer classes. Because no special network is required beyond an HTML internet browser, classes can be accessed from any computer anywhere in the world, and supplies time- flexible courses that can be taken anytime as long as the course is posted on the internet. VLE incorporates audio, animation, video, and text in a multimedia computer environment (Goldber & McKhann, 2000).

VLEs are not computer microworlds, computer aided instruction (CAI), or classroom-based learning environments where students are in a self-contained computer-based learning environment (CBLE) without any interactions with other participants or where teachers employ various technologies as tools to support classroom activities (Piccoli et al., 2001).

The VLE is the core component of distance learning or blended learning instruction environments (Educause Center for Applied Research, 2003). The distance learning approach depends on internet communication between the instructor and the student where the instructor provides all the necessary course materials, students download or stream the course materials, and students are assessed with a variety of different techniques designed specifically for this purpose.

Science and other technical subjects are more difficult to teach online because of the laboratory requirements. However, some researchers have found that virtual labs are as effective as classroom laboratory settings for teaching students concepts that will prepare them for actual laboratory research. iLabCentral, is one example of a virtual lab product that delivers high quality lab experiences in a VLE. Proponents suggest that virtual labs give students access to equipment they may not have in a traditional classroom and instructors no longer have to set up and clean up after a science experiment (Le Roux & Evans, 2011). (AR)

Educause Center for Applied Research. (2003). *Faculty use of course management systems (Volume 2)*. Boulder, CO: G. Morgan.

Goldber, H. R., & McKhann, G. M. (2000, June). Student test scores are improved in a virtual learning environment, *Advances in Physiology Education, 23*(1), 59-66.

Kumar, A., Pakala, R., Ragade, R. K., & Wong, J. P. (1998). The virtual learning environment system. *Proceedings of the Frontiers in Education Conference, 2*, 711-716.

Le Roux, C. J. B., & Evans, N. (2011). Can cloud computing bridge the digital divide in South African secondary education? *Information Development, 27*(2), 109-116.

Piccoli, G. Ahmad, R., & Ives, B. (2001). Web-based virtual learning environments: A research framework and a preliminary assessment of effectiveness in basic IT skills training. *MIS Quarterly, 25*(4), 401-426.

Printed in the United States
By Bookmasters